Paul's Gender Theology and the Ordained Women's Ministry in the CCAP in Zambia

Copyright 2021 Lazarus Chilenje

All rights reserved. No part of this publication may be reproduced, stored in a retrieval system, or transmitted in any form or by any means, electronic, mechanical, photocopying, recording or otherwise without prior permission from the publishers.

Published by
Mzuni Press
P/Bag 201 Luwinga
Mzuzu 2
Malawi

ISBN   978-99960-60-92-2

eISBN   978-99960-60-93-3

Mzuni Press is represented outside Malawi by:

African Books Collective Oxford (orders@africanbookscollective.com)

www.mzunipress.blogspot.com
www.africanbookscollective.com

Editorial assistance: Hope Kaombe

Cover: Josephine Kawejere

Paul's Gender Theology and the Ordained Women's Ministry in the CCAP in Zambia

Lazarus Chilenje

Mzuni Books no. 48
Mzuzu
2021

Dedication

I dedicate this work to my wife, Shera Sakala-Chilenje, who has lovingly stood by my side all these years of my studies, and to our three wonderful children: Victor Chilenje, Richard (Joseph) Chilenje and our little girl Mervis Chilenje.

Acknowledgements

First and foremost, in a special way, I extend my sincere and heartfelt thanks and appreciation to my beloved supervisor, Associate Professor Jonathan Samuel Nkhoma, who has tirelessly helped me at every stage of the research. When I stood on the threshold of the building of Gender Theology in Pauline Literature, Associate Professor Jonathan Nkhoma was the one who provided a map I could not have found on my own. His vast knowledge of New Testament and non-Theological disciplines prevented me from getting lost. His genuine loyalty to students allowed me to wander on my own, and this is how I discovered the fun of doing research. I truly appreciate him for his patience, love, generosity, guidance and constructive criticism.

I acknowledge gratefully the contribution of Professor Dr Klaus Fiedler who assisted me from the inception of the topic of my study before I was assigned to Associate Professor Jonathan Nkhoma as my supervisor up to the completion of this dissertation. Professor Klaus Fiedler challenged me to remain focused on the subject and recommended books to make this project relevant. I am indeed grateful for his guidance and constructive criticism. I am also grateful to Dr Rachel NyaGondwe Fiedler for the encouragement and a source of inspiration to pursue studies on women. Her writings on women's need for liberation indeed motivated me.

Special thanks also go to the Presbyterian Church of the United States of America (PCUSA) Leadership International Development, for their continued financial assistance for the period of four years. May God richly bless the PCUSA Louisville office via Mrs Nancy J. Collins, Regional Liaison for East Central Africa. Also, I am grateful to Nancy for editing my first draft of this work. I will always live to remember her gesture.

I am greatly indebted to CCAP Zambia for allowing me to study with Mzuzu University even at times when I was required to discharge certain duties.

I thank all those who contributed to my research when I looked for information. I am grateful in particular to Rev M.R. Kabandama, General Secretary of CCAP Zambia for not only allowing me to conduct research in the Congregations and Presbyteries but also sending questionnaires to Synod Executive members. I sincerely thank all those I have not mentioned by name but have immensely contributed to my studies up to this end.

I also thank my wife Shera, sons Victor and Richard, and daughter Mervis for being patient, cheerful, supportive and flexible while I was busy with my 'book thing.' Also, when I worked during odd hours of the night and travelled for weeks to Mzuzu University. Shera, our relationship proves to me that it is true relationships that are a source of healing.

Glory to the Triune God, the Father, the Son and the Holy Spirit!

Lazarus Chilenje, -April 2020

Abbreviations

CCAPZ:	Church of Central Africa, Presbyterian Zambia
CCAPLA:	CCAP Synod of Livingstonia Archives
CLAIM:	Christian Literature Association in Malawi
JETS:	Journal of the Evangelical Theological Society
JMTUC:	Justo Mwale Theological University College
JMU:	Justo Mwale University
MZUNI:	Mzuzu University
NT:	New Testament
PCUSA:	Presbyterian Church of United States of America
UPCSA:	Uniting Presbyterian Church in Southern Africa

Table of Contents

Chapter 1	9
Introduction	9
Chapter 2	13
The Provision of Space for Women Leadership in CCAP Zambia	13
Chapter 3	51
The Place of Women in the Greco-Roman World	51
Chapter 4	79
Gender Theology in Pauline Literature	79
Chapter 5	142
Toward a Theology of Gender in CCAP Zambia	142
Bibliography	147

Chapter 1

Introduction

The Bible is the foundational document for Christianity. Indeed, 'the Bible is the engine that is keeping the church running."[1] The Bible is central in Christian life and is daily used by Christians all over the world. Despite the fact that the Bible is widely honoured as the soul of theology[2] by Christians, it has not contributed to unifying adherents of the Christian faith. This could be attributed to divergent interpretations of the Bible. One major contributing factor is probably how the Bible is interpreted.

People using the same source of knowledge arrive at different conclusions. With numerous problems faced in the continent, the Word of God is regarded as a source of answers and even of solutions to all the mind-boggling questions and experiences. Indeed, in the Bible the people of Africa find hope and answer as to the meaning of life. The mere fact that users of the same book arrive at widely different conclusions requires scholars to investigate critically what constitutes a responsible reading of the Bible.

The word of God has some passages that are relatively easy to interpret as well as others that are difficult. Many Bible readers find texts, especially those written by Paul, among other writers, difficult. This calls for scholarly work which will enable members of the church to understand the Bible and avoid polarizing opinions. The debate has become completely polarized in the treatment of many writers for whom there are just two sides: those who oppose the participation of

---

[1] Hilary Mijoga, "Bible and Church Growth in Malawi," *Religion in Malawi*, no. 8, 1998, pp. 27-33 [p. 27].

[2] Joseph A. Fitzmyer, *Scripture, the Soul of Theology*, Nairobi: Paulist Press, 2005 (1994).

women in ministry, and those who support it.[3] This research intends to wrestle with Pauline passages on women in the letters written to the Corinthian and Ephesian churches in light of Galatians 3:28, and to relate this to the role of women in the Church of Central Africa, Presbyterian Synod of Zambia (CCAP Zambia) today.

The CCAP Zambia resolved to ordain women to the Holy Ministry in 2002. In spite of this resolution there are still church members and male theologians who think that women should only take supportive roles in the Church. As such women's participation is not fully being realized. The foregoing situation may be due to cultural inclinations hard to unlearn or misunderstanding of scripture such as those written by Paul to the Corinthian and Ephesians Churches.

Everywhere, in Africa as much as in the rest of the world, the danger of cultural reading exists, but the Bible has proved, in the long run, to be able to put up quite some resistance to such cultural reading and has often hit back after periods of cultural suppression of part of its message to challenge what seemed to be the consensus of the custodians of its message.[4]

I am a member and ordained minister of the CCAP Zambia, and a lecturer at Chasefu Theological College. I have actually experienced and observed gender imbalances of women vying for Holy Ministry in the church, and I want to offer CCAP Zambia members an understanding of gender equality based on Paul's' theology in the passages traditionally seen to bar women from church participation on an equal basis with men. Special emphasis is placed on 1Cor 11:2-16, 1Cor 14:34-35, 1Tim 2:11-12 in light of Galatians 3:28 with regard to the role of women.

---

[3] Stanley Grenz and D. Kjesbo, *Women in the Church*, Downers Grove: IVP, 1995, pp. 18, 33.

[4] Klaus Fiedler, "Gender Equality in the New Testament: The Case of St Paul," *Religion in Malawi*, no. 1, 2003, pp. 19-36 [p. 19].

There are two major approaches: Egalitarians and Complementarians.[5] Christian Egalitarians are those who conclude in their Scripture interpretation that the teaching of Jesus and the apostle Paul abolished gender-specific roles both in church and family. They base their teaching on many facts, one of them is that both men and women were created equal by God (Gen 1:27) and that neither man nor woman were cursed by God at the fall of man (Gen 3:16). Also, Jesus' radical view of the new covenant in relation to women was affirmed by the apostle Paul when he said that there is no male or female, you are all equal in Christ (Gal 3:28).[6] I subscribe to this approach.

Complementarians believe that God made men and women equal in personhood and value but different in roles. They understand the Bible as teaching that God gave men and women different roles in the church because of their maleness (male nature) and femaleness (female nature),[7] but such differences do not imply superiority or inferiority.[8] In the quest to deal with the perceived difficult Pauline passages under study in this project in light of Galatians 3:28, a hermeneutical method will be employed. While all hermeneutical methods aim at the correct interpretation of a biblical passage, I will use the Historical-Exegetical Method. In recent decades, the most prominent method in biblical studies has been known as the Historical-Critical Method. While the Historical-Critical Method remains famous and useful, and while the present study has benefited from its insights, the approach, taken in this study, however, is that Historical-Exegetical method where meaning is

---

[5] Ibid, p. 11.

[6] Samuel Koranteng-Pipim, *Receiving the Word. How New Approaches to the Bible Impact Our Biblical Faith and Lifestyle*, Michigan: Berean Books, 1996, pp. 26-30.

[7] See: John Koessler, "Wounds of a Friend: Complementarians," *Christianity Today*, vol. 52, no. 6, June 2008.

[8] Samuele Bacchiocchi, *Women in the Church: A Biblical Study on the Role of Women in the Church,* Berrien Springs: Biblical Perspectives, 1987, p. 126.

determined through a historical study of the biblical context coupled with an exegetical analysis of the relevant texts, while also drawing some insights from the Literary Analytical Method.

Although the church officially ordains women in CCAP Zambia, there are still two positions among the members of the church. It is therefore imperative to understand Pauline texts in light of Historical-Critical approach to appreciate the need for the ordination of women in the Church.

Chapter 2

The Provision of Space for Women Leadership in CCAP Zambia

Introduction

This chapter explains the contemporary context of the church now that women have been accepted to the ordained ministry and the factors that discourage women from applying even when the doors are now open. There are many women who serve as elders and deacons in the church, but the same is not true when it comes to Holy Ministry since for a long time women were denied entry into the ordained ministry. The issue of leadership is discussed with reference to ordination but does not include women elders and other top positions in the Synod.

Women leadership is one of the widest discussed subjects in both secular and Christian sectors. Women are said to be fighting for liberation in the area of leadership. The Church has not been left out in this fight for liberation. There are some who think that women's ministry should be limited while others are of the opinion that women's ministry should not be limited. Initially in CCAP Zambia, women were limited in the service of God's work and it was not until 2002 that they were allowed to be ordained as church ministers.[1] For a long time the CCAP Zambia would not allow ordination of women due to various reasons that ranged from theological to cultural.

---

[1] The term minister focuses on the ministry of preaching and teaching of the Word of God. They are defined as those who are appointed to particular congregations where they rule by the word of God over those placed in their charge. They are called ministers because of their service and office.

Brief History of CCAP Zambia

The CCAP Zambia traces its origin from Livingstonia Mission of the Free Church of Scotland that was formed in memory of Dr David Livingstone in 1874, who died in 1873 at Chitambo (Zambia) after his three missionary and exploration journeys.[2]

Following the death of this great missionary and explorer, the formation of Livingstonia Mission was the result of the initiative of Rev Dr James Steward of Lovedale, in South Africa. While attending the Free Church of Scotland General Assembly in May 1874, he suggested the establishment of the Livingstonia Mission in memory of the late Dr David Livingstone's work in Central Africa. Steward proposed the establishment of an institution, "both Industrial and Educational to teach the truth of the arts of civilized life and the Gospel to the natives of the country. The institution which shall be placed on a carefully selected and commanding spot in Central Africa be called Livingstonia."[3]

On 12th May, 1875, the first missionary party left Scotland for Lake Nyasa (Malawi). There were seven: E.D. Young in charge as the leader; Robert Laws, ordained medical missionary, second in command and lent to the Free Church Mission by the United Presbyterian Church; George Johnston, carpenter; John M. Fadyen, first engineer/blacksmith; Allan Simpson, second engineer; Alexander Riddell, agriculturist; and William Baker, seaman. To make the Livingstonia Mission as effective as possible, a small steamer, the Ilala, capable of being dismantled, was built for their use.[4]

---

[2] Robert Laws, *Reminiscences of Livingstonia*, Edinburgh: Oliver and Boyd, 1934, p. 6.

[3] John McCracken, *Politics and Christianity in Malawi, 1875-1940: The Impact of the Livingstonia Mission in the Northern Province*, Blantyre: CLAIM, 2000, pp. 47-117.

[4] Ibid.

After reaching Cape Maclear in Chief Mponda's area, on Sunday the 17th October 1875, E.D. Young established the Livingstonia Mission Station there. The Rev Dr James Stewart, who was to take over the leadership from Young arrived in October 1876 with a party of five, one man from Scotland, Dr William Black, and four teachers/evangelists (Mapasa Ntintili, Isaac Wauchope, Shadrack Mngunana and William Koyi) from Lovedale in South Africa.[5] However, Cape Maclear proved to be unhealthy. At the end of five years there were five missionary graves, but only ninety pupils in the mission school and one baptized convert, Albert Namalambe, who was later put in charge of the mission, after Dr and Mrs Laws had moved to Bandawe on 29th March, 1881. At Bandawe, Chiefs Malenga Mzoma, Chimbano, Khwalala, Chiweyu, Yakucha and Chikhokho cordially welcomed the missionaries. They were chiefs of the Banda clan, generally known as Kapunda Banda.[6] The missionaries called the place Bandawe where a hospital, school blocks, a carpentry shop and gardens were established. Religious worship and instructions were carried out as part of every department. From Bandawe in 1894 the headquarter of the Mission moved to Kondowe (the third Livingstonia) where the Overtoun Institution became the training centre. People trained at Bandawe were sent to different places for evangelism. These included Karonga District to the north, Kasungu in central Malawi, the Northern Province of Zambia, the Central Province and also Marambo in the present day Eastern Province of Zambia (Chipata, Lundazi and Chama districts), as well as Southern Tanzania.[7]

Following the conducive environment at Bandawe and Khondowe in the early years of the mission's existence, ten mission stations were

---

[5] Ibid.

[6] Victor Chilenje, "The Origin and Development of Church of Central Africa Presbyterian in Zambia 1882-2004," DTh, University of Stellenbosch, 2007, p. 21.

[7] Ibid.

established in Zambia. From 1881 to 1912, extensive mission and evangelistic work was embarked upon among the Tumbuka, Senga, Bemba, Namwanga, Lala, Chewa, Ngoni and Bisa. The mission stations were: Mwenzo (1882), Chitheba (1882), Uyombe (1889), Tamanda (1894), Kamoto (1896), Kazembe (1897), Lubwa (1904), Chitambo (1907), Chasefu (1922), and Lundazi (1962).[8] Robert Laws lived to his word of establishing a mission which was to be evangelistic, educational and industrial, and work progressed well. This dissertation will focus on the first one, evangelistic.

Unlike today, during Laws' time, baptism was only granted after a long rigorous period of church education, and ordination was only conferred after a long period of probation after completion of theological training. Even though Livingstonia was established in 1875, it was only in 1921 that the Free Church of Scotland ordained its first three indigenous Zambian ministers: Yonah Lengwe Mvula, Simeon K. Ngulube and Euwen Siwale. Victor Chilenje compiled a list of Africans ordained as CCAP ministers and all ministers are male, from the 1940s up to 1982.[9]

Women in CCAP Zambia

Women have been serving as church elders since the birth of CCAP Zambia. This is because Livingstonia Synod started ordaining women as elders soon after the CCAP was formed on the 16th September, 1924, when Blantyre and Livingstonia Presbyteries came together.[10] Elders form part of the Kirk session which is the governing body of the church which follows a Presbyterian form of church government. Since women have been attending and participating in session meetings to which they are full members, serving at the Holy Communion, representing the

---

[8] Ibid.

[9] Victor Chilenje, "A History of the Church of Central Africa Presbyterian (CCAP) in Zambia 1880s-1998," BTh, JMTC, 1998, p. 65.

[10] Ibid, p. 87.

congregation at Presbytery and Synod meetings and also shepherding the Christian community, one can say that women were and are actively involved in the leadership ministry of the church except ordination to Holy Ministry.

In CCAP Zambia, women are the majority, but very few of them are ministers. However, most elders and deacons are women.[11] I can therefore confidently conclude that women are included in the decision-making process because in Presbyterian polity, elders and deacons form what is known as the Kirk session which is the governing body of the church. It is worth mentioning that deacons do not have the right to vote during the Kirk Session, it is only the elders who are allowed to vote on issues when the need arises. Presbyterians like the idea of church rule by limited groups of office-bearers. Their adage is "a few of the best rule the rest."[12] Presbyterianism is a form of church government ruled by elders. Van Wyk writes that for this reason "the qualification of the ministers of a religious community is of vital importance to the validity of its government."[13] There is one office of the presbyter with two parts, namely "teaching elder or Minister and ruling elder-the laity."[14] Crucial decisions are made at the session level.

---

[11] "Update of the Life and Work of the CCAP Synod of Zambia," A report presented to Presbyterian Church United States of America (PCUSA) Congregations and Outreach Foundation, September to November, 2014, p. 15.

[12] Steven Paas, *Ministers and Elders: The Birth of Presbyterianism*, Zomba: Kachere, 2007, p. 9.

[13] Jurgens Johannes van Wyk, *The Historical Development of the Offices according to the Presbyterian Tradition of Scotland*, Zomba: Kachere, 2004, p. 111.

[14] Ibid, p. 119.

Women can serve as Vestry[15] Chairpersons. A Vestry Chairperson is supposed to be an elder. Since women can be chosen as church elders they are also eligible for positions of chairperson, secretary, and treasurer in a particular prayer house. It is important to note that very few female elders are included in the executive committees of the Kirk Sessions, the Presbyteries the Synod.[16] Since its inception, only one woman has served as a Synod executive member in the CCAP Zambia.[17] In the case of female ministers, many have held positions at Presbytery level as moderators or Presbytery clerks. It is also important to point out that female ministers have held positions of coordinators of Women's Guild and of Community Schools Department at Synod level. However, women have enjoyed leadership in leading other women in Christian Women's Guild (popularly known as Umanyano in Tumbuka) which gathers every Friday for Bible Study.[18] Women have found consolation in expressing their leadership roles in this Christian Women's Guild. The first woman to lead women's ministry was Catherine Mazunda Nkhata. At the Synod level, the only woman who held the position of Executive member was Betty Mvula Mtonga. She was among the ten decision makers of the Synod.[19]

Ordination of Women in CCAP Zambia

Women are playing a vital role in the Church even though their involvement in decision-making bodies is limited. Women are least represented in this area because this engagement is linked to administering

---

[15] A vestry is the lowest court of elders and deacons which runs the affairs of a prayer house. A congregation is composed of prayer houses and every prayer house is administered by elders and deacons, and these form a vestry.

[16] *Practice and Procedure of CCAP Synod of Zambia*, Lusaka, 2012, p. 39.

[17] Int. Rev David Chiboboka, CTC Principal, Lundazi, 15.5.2015.

[18] Int. Rev Dr Victor Chilenje, Synod Moderator, Justo Mwale University, Lusaka, 10.7.2015.

[19] Ibid. 10.5.2015.

the sacraments. There are cultural and theological reasons that are used to deter women from participating in such a role. The issue of concern to feminist ecclesiology is indeed the position and ministry of women in the church. As Susan Rakoczy has pointed out, no issue in feminist theology is as contentious as that of women's place in the church and their call to ministry.[20] Similarly, Anne Clifford admits that the topic of women's participation in their churches is such a big issue that it can only be adequately covered in many volumes.[21] It is a controversial issue because, as Nicola Slee has also observed, until women speak up, many congregations will continue to deny women access to its practices, offices and positions of leadership, as well as opportunities for theological study.[22]

The discussion of the ordination of women to Holy Ministry began within the CCAP Synod of Livingstonia before the CCAP Zambia won its autonomy.[23] It was during Rev Wedson P. Chibambo's tenure as General Secretary (1978-1988) that the issue of women's ordination as ministers cropped up again and again.[24] Women were now interested in theological training and, as a result of this, a desire to become ministers was born. The struggle went on for a number of years, and the victory only came well after Rev Chibambo's tenure. It should be noted that

---

[20] Susan Rakoczy, *In Her Name: Women Doing Theology*, Pietermaritzburg: Cluster, 2004, p. 198.

[21] Anne M. Clifford, *Introducing Feminist Theology*, Maryknoll: Orbis, 2001, p. 148.

[22] Nicola Slee, *Faith and Feminism: An Introduction to Christian Feminist Theology*, London: Darton, Longman and Todd, 2003, p. 105.

[23] Minutes Chasefu Presbytery, 17th-21st June 1981, Minutes of Chasefu Presbytery of the Church of Central Africa Presbyterian Synod of Livingstonia 17th -21st June 1981 CCAPLA.

[24] For his life and ministry source: Chance Mwangombo, "The Life and Work of the Rev Wedson Paul Chibambo and Lucy Chibambo of the CCAP Synod of Livingstonia," BTh, University of Livingstonia, 2013.

during these discussions elders and ministers from CCAP Zambia were in attendance.

A careful look at the minutes of GAC held at Ekwendeni Lay Training Centre in Malawi from 9th to 11th March, 1983 unearths the following views of members:

> That the subject was premature, that it was against our tradition, that there was no theological reason to deny women to be ordained and that already the Synod accepts women to the eldership.[25]

The issue of ordination of women to Holy Ministry appeared again on the 1984 Synod agenda. The Synod discussed and resolved the following:

> A study of the traditional view of the Livingstonia Synod was to be done, the Theological and Biblical warrant for and against should be looked into and the social warrant for or against should be surveyed.[26]

In view of this, the issue was pushed to further research. In 1986, the issue of ordination of women was discussed again. A request was presented to admit women to the Holy Ministry. The Synod agreed to this in principle and agreed to refer the matter to the congregations through the presbyteries. The reports from presbyteries were to be presented to the next General Administration Committee meeting (GAC).[27] After hearing the reports from presbyteries during the GAC in the following year 1987, the committee resolved that time had not yet

---

[25] Victor Chilenje, "The Origin and Development of Church of Central Africa Presbyterian in Zambia 1882-2004," DTh, University of Stellenbosch, 2007, p. 221.

[26] Minutes of General Administration Committee of 3-7 April 1984.

[27] Minutes of the General Administration Committee of 16-20 April 1985 minute 1315/85.

come to ordain women to the Holy Ministry, so the issue was pended for future consideration.[28]

During the Livingstonia Synod conference in 1992,[29] it was approved that women could be ordained. At this point people were free to do theological training regardless of gender.

One of the critical issues the CCAP Zambia has struggled with since its inception is the ordination of women to the Holy Ministry, which began with Livingstonia Synod before Zambia was given a status of a Synod. It should be noted that this time still CCAP Zambia was not given the autonomy. It can then be rightly argued that CCAP Zambia never engaged itself to look at this issue of ordination of women. At the time, there were only four ordained ministers and two missionary ministers from Livingstonia Synod, one of whom was later to become the first General Secretary of CCAP Zambia on 28th October, 1984.[30] I argue therefore that this issue has indeed never been discussed in the CCAP Zambia context but heavily relied on the decisions of Livingstonia Synod.

Since the Livingstonia Synod accepted ordination of Women to Holy Ministry, the CCAP Zambia at its Synod meeting of 2002[31] took the challenge of accepting ordination of women. This was motivated by the wind of change in Livingstonia Synod and Paul's theology that "there is neither Jew nor Greek, there is neither bond nor free, there is neither male nor female: for we are all one in Christ Jesus" (Gal 3:26-29).

---

[28] Minutes of the General Administration Committee of 1-5 April 1992.

[29] Minutes 29/92 of the CCAP Livingstonia Synod of 18-23 August, 1992.

[30] Rev W.K. Jele was the first General Secretary of CCAP Zambia in 1984. He was a missionary from Malawi. For his life story see: Kelly Bwalya, *The Life of Dr Wyson Moses Kauzobofa Jele. Missionary to Zambia*, Mzuzu: Mzuni Press, 2014, ²2017.

[31] Minutes of the 10th CCAP Zambia Synod held at Lundazi Boma from 20th to 25th August, 2002, pp. 46-48.

Following this text many sincere persons concluded that the new dispensation has obliterated all the distinctions: that now believers occupy exactly the same position before God and are equally free to exercise all the functions of the entire body.[32] This was a big milestone for the Church and those women who had already done theology were motivated to be ordained as ministers.

Women in Holy Ministry

CCAP Zambia Synod has the following women serving in the Holy Ministry.

Kondwani Nkhoma

Kondwani Nkhoma went for theological training at Zomba Theological College 1994-1997 and ended up working as a women's coordinator.[33] Before going for training, she was a teacher by profession. It is interesting to note that people saw in Kondwani a minister in 1977, but her parents declined due to the minimal salary received by a Holy Minister and the patriarchal cultural influence from her family. After the Synod accepted the ordination of women in 2002, she became the first woman to be licensed and given a congregation on 25th August 2002. She recalls many women and men did not appreciate this call and as such she had to work extra hard in her first small rural congregation. "I could cycle fifty kilometers for session meetings to prove my critics wrong. I served in this congregation for six years before being moved to yet another small urban congregation."[34] She further observes that all of the three congregations the Synod sent her to serve were small in size without infrastructure for either church building or manse. "At the

---

[32] Ibid, pp. 46-48.

[33] Int. Rev S.M. Mithi, First Synod Moderator CCAPZ, Chipata CCAP Congregation, 22.5.2015.

[34] Int. Rev Kondwani Nkhoma, Kalulushi CCAP Congregation, Kalulushi Copperbelt, 24.5.2015.

current Kalulushi congregation, even the junior minister could not be sustained but the Synod decided to send her there anyway. I was sent to Kalulushi congregation when the congregation failed to sustain a male junior Minister. The Synod seems to exhibit a bias towards men."[35] But through God's grace, the congregation is now doing very fine numerically, spiritually, financially and also developmentally.

Despite serving prudently, many men and women continued to look down upon her. At the Synod, men commented negatively and also harshly towards female folk. "This explains why my being ordained took two years instead of the normal one-year probation. I was only ordained on 29th August, 2004."[36] Most issues affecting women are thrown out without love, care and understanding by Church courts making it very difficult for women to create space for women leadership. Rev Nkhoma has served as Presbytery Moderator and Clerk which positions came about because of presbyteries that are constituted of only three or four congregations—in some cases with only three ministers. According to Rev Nkhoma these positions would still be occupied by men had it not been for these phenomena. Because of her experience as a teacher, the position she has held on merit is that of being part-time Coordinator Community Schools in CCAP Zambia.

According to Nkhoma very few men at the Synod level appreciate what women are doing after exceeding their expectations. Nkhoma argues this makes female ministers work in panic thereby straining them to prove to men their capabilities. It is believed that women cannot handle certain duties such as administration of Holy Communion, due to menstruation. In addition, women were not seen as suitable for the position of the teaching Elder because at times a woman would become pregnant and this would make the pulpit work look awkward. It is interesting to note that women are considered unholy to administer

---

[35] Ibid.
[36] Ibid.

Holy Communion due to menstruation, but the same women serve at the Holy Communion as elders, being actively involved in the preparation of the elements for the Holy Communion.

The journey towards making gender balance a women's agenda in CCAP Zambia has a long way to go. Rev Nkhoma attributes this to women themselves not supporting each other to push this agenda forward. Women are generally not supportive of each other and are enemies to themselves. It is against this background that the ratio between men and women in terms of going to Synod or Presbytery meetings is very bad. Men always outnumber women during Presbytery and Synod meetings. This, according to Nkhoma, disadvantages women when it comes to passing certain policies that require voting. "Even at the lowest court called session, women lack capability and education to hold administrative positions since many women can hardly read and write."[37] But Rev Nkhoma was quick to point out that women not only need education but also exposure to liberate themselves from the fear of the unknown, and from the perception that only men make good leaders. But for her, she has fought a good fight of faith and finished her race, hence she was looking forward to retirement in 2016 from active participation in Holy Ministry (1 Timothy 4:6-8). She passed away on 29th June 2015. She will be remembered as the first CCAP Zambia woman to take up the challenge to be ordained to the Holy Ministry - indeed influenced by Pauline theology of equal participation in the ordained ministry.[38]

Thandiwe Chipeta (nee Theu)

The first woman to go into theological college on her own account in CCAP Zambia was Thandiwe Theu Chipeta. According to Thandiwe

---

[37] Int. Rev Kondwani Nkhoma, Kalulushi CCAP Congregation, Kalulushi Copperbelt, 24.5.2015.

[38] Int. Rev M.R. Kabandama, General Secretary, Synod Offices, Lusaka, 17.7.2015.

Chipeta she was privileged to be removed from a class of pastors' wives to do theology alongside her husband whom the church had sent to college. She did her theological training at Justo Mwale Theological College 1995-1998. At the time Livingstonia Synod had already accepted Ordination to Holy Ministry for women and CCAP Zambia was still debating the issue. She found herself doing theology at the time the wind of change at Justo Mwale had reached its peak promoting feminist theology. She recalls "I found challenges whilst in college. Male students could not accept that a woman can do theology. Men argued that culturally women are considered unclean during menstruation and at home they can't even add salt to the relish. Also, biblically women are considered unclean, hence how would you ascend to the pulpit and administer Holy Communion or even preach." "As a married female Minister, how are you going to balance between home and ministry?" they challenged.[39] Responding to the question "Have men fully accepted women to Holy Ministry?" Chipeta answered that ten per cent (10%) have accepted. Many male ministers and the laity in leadership positions have not accepted female ministers. When it came for her to do her five weeks practical and trial sermon, the then General Secretary responded that "We don't know that person."[40] Because of this she did her practical and trial sermon with the Uniting Presbyterian Church of Southern Africa. But men and women laity not in leadership positions have accepted females to ordained ministry. She recalls "It took five years after graduation before being accepted into Holy Ministry."[41] It is this kind of attitude by those in leadership that makes women's participation in Holy Ministry difficult. There is no spirit of inclusiveness.

---

[39] Int. Rev T.T. Chipeta, Chitala CCAP Congregation, Lundazi, 21.5.2015.

[40] Ibid, 21.5.2015.

[41] Ibid, 21.5.2015.

However, a second milestone was achieved at the Synod meeting[42] when she was licensed as a Minister of Word and Sacrament on 29th August 2004, on the same day Rev Nkhoma Kondwani was ordained. This inclusiveness and participation of women has challenged the doubting Thomas' belief in gender equality.[43]

After being licensed, Rev Chipeta was posted to a small urban congregation as the first minister there. She ministered in three small urban congregations before the synod decided to send her to a small rural congregation. All of these congregations are now viable unlike when she was first sent to them.[44] There is a phenomenon that can be contrasted here that—like the first woman minister—Thandiwe Chipeta has also served in congregations that are small but after serving there they are now doing fine. It appears women are currently performing well in terms of ministry. This shows some levels of competency of women leadership.

Thandiwe Chipeta has held positions of Presbytery Moderator and Clerk. The later position helped her to see how resistant men are to fully accept women to the ordained ministry. At session level, most executive members are men and if they are dictators in their homes, they cannot accept to be led by a female minister. Worse still, if a woman is in a leadership position—either Presbytery Moderator or Clerk—male ministers and laity do not consider female ministers to be wise. This she attributes to the patriarchal culture that promotes the status quo of male-centredness. She observed that in CCAP Zambia no female minister has ever been an executive member except for one female elder, Betty Mvula Mtonga. But after divorcing her husband in a secular

---

[42] Minutes of the 11th Synod meeting held at Chipata Teachers Training College from 24th to 29th August, 2004, pp. 11-12.

[43] Int. Thandiwe Chipeta, Chitala CCAP Congregation, Lundazi, 21.5.2015.

[44] Ibid, p. 12.

court of law, men are using her divorce arguing that all women are failures.⁴⁵

Gertrude Banda (nee Nyirenda)

Gertrude Nyirenda Banda was trained at Chasefu Theological College as the third woman in CCAP Zambia. She was trained at Chasefu when it informally opened in 2007 with an intake of sixteen evangelists as students. She graduated in 2009 with a licentiate in theology.⁴⁶ She has since served in three rural congregations in the eastern part of Zambia. She has held positions of Presbytery Moderator and Advisor of Christian Women's Guild.⁴⁷ She observed that ordained ministry has not been easy for one simple reason: that men and women have not fully accepted women in ordained ministry. "These people feel women cannot be ministers."⁴⁸ They argue that female ministers are not competent enough to handle the ordained ministry due to menstruation. Others argue that Jesus had no female disciples or their reason is based on Paul's injunctions on women. She observes that patrilineal culture is strongly at play in the minds of many Christians. This phenomenon has led to women not supporting each other. She argues that there is a lot of inferiority complex and jealousy amongst women. Women feel only men can make good leaders as they are the head of the family. This scenario prevents both women and men from according female ministers the respect they deserve.⁴⁹ Unless women rise to the occasion and support each other, they cannot win the battle of gender equality and equity. But she was quick to point out that most Pauline

---

[45] Int. Thandiwe Chipeta, Chitala CCAP Congregation, Lundazi, 21.5.2015.

[46] Int. Rev Dr V. Chilenje, Synod Moderator, Justo Mwale University, Lusaka, 17.8.2015.

[47] Ibid, 17.8.2015.

[48] Int. Rev Getrude N. Banda, Chasefu CCAP Congregation, Lundazi, 24.5.2015.

[49] Ibid, 24.5.2015.

writings are literalistically interpreted to mean that they bar women from the ordained ministry. Yet Galatians 3:28 is liberative.[50]

Susan Nyirenda (nee Tembo)

The fourth woman to go into theological training in CCAP Zambia was Susan Nyirenda.[51] The Church sent her to Justo Mwale Theological University College in 2008. She completed her Bachelor of Theology (BTh) in 2011. Together with her husband, the Synod sent her to the Copperbelt where she is the minister of Luanshya CCAP Congregation. She is the Coordinator of the Synod Christian Women's Guild and Presbytery Moderator.[52] But she argues that there is serious resistance by both men and women to these leadership positions. According to her, men traditionally are not used to being led by women. They feel it is a humiliation and fail to open up on most issues affecting them. There is a leadership crisis in the Synod due to the status quo. Since most positions are held by men even at the lowest courts, there is a challenge for female ministers to instruct men on what they should do in those positions. She further argues that most men stigmatize female ministers due to cultural beliefs and biblical decrees, especially passages of Paul and the Levitical codes. Women are still considered unclean, are considered to be possessions and should be submissive to their husbands, who are the head of the family.[53]

However, some men have started accepting women in ordained ministry due to the influence of Pauline theology, especially Gal 3:26-

---

[50] Ibid.

[51] Int. Rev M.R. Kabandama, General Secretary, Synod Offices, Lusaka, 17.8.2015.

[52] Ibid, 18.8.2015.

[53] Int. Susan Tembo Nyirenda, Luanshya CCAP Congregation, Luanshya, 24.5.2015.

29.⁵⁴ But fellow women have lagged behind in this matter. They are not supportive of female ministers because they are not used to experiencing female leadership. Also, women are jealous of each other and have no trust in women leadership. Female ministers are said to lack diligence and competency, as well as administrative and negotiating skills. In view of that, women have no representation in Synod leadership even as executive members and therefore issues affecting women are not addressed adequately.[55]

It is this kind of phenomenon that prevents women from being active in decision making. But she argued that women have proved their potential. They have performed very well in congregations previously led by men who had left them behind struggling, and the women ministers have succeeded in achieving viability in all areas.[56]

Naomi Daka

Naomi Daka also went for theological training at Chasefu Theological College in 2010.[57] At that time, the institution was formally opened with an intake of twelve students. She was the only female student among these twelve.[58] Daka received challenges from male students whilst in college. They were skeptical not only on her being single, but also that women cannot rule a man.[59] After she graduated in 2012 with a Diploma in Theology, Daka was sent to the southern part of Zambia to a small congregation called Mazabuka.[60] She is the Presbytery Clerk and the

---

[54] Ibid, 24.5.2015.

[55] Ibid, 24.5.2015.

[56] Ibid.

[57] Int. Rev David Chiboboka, CTC Principal, Lundazi, 30.7.2015.

[58] Ibid.

[59] Ibid.

[60] Int. Rev M. R. Kabandama, General Secretary, Synod Offices, Lusaka, 17.8.2015.

Youth Advisor in the David Livingstone Presbytery.[61] She argues that both men and women are resistant to her being a minister there. She reports discouraging sentiments "I cannot be ruled by a woman."[62] One male minister also said "The five female ministers are already enough, they have failed. If this enrolment is left unchecked, the church will be led by incompetent women."[63]

This resistance goes to show that women have not been fully received both by men and fellow women. She observed that there is a philosophy of cultural and biblical tenets especially based on the Levitical code. In view of that, most positions are held by men in the church. However, according to scripture, in Christ there is neither male nor female- we are all one in Christ Jesus. Galatians 3:26-29 is a comfort to her. The same God who called men is the one who also called her. There is gender equality on the basis of us being in Christ; hence there should be no discrimination.[64]

Church Leaders' Perceptions on Female Ministers

It is evident that these women ministers are slowly creating space in ordained ministry and also in leadership. While some men and women look at them with pride in congregations and presbyteries where they are serving, it is important also to find out how the church leadership and fellow women leaders perceive them. It can be argued from their responses there is some degree of skepticism.

---

[61] Ibid, 17.8.2015.

[62] Rev Naomi Daka, Mazabuka CCAP Congregation, Mazabuka, Southern Province, 18.5.2015.

[63] Ibid.

[64] Ibid.

Synod Leaders' Responses

A total of 27 Synod leaders past and present[65] throughout the country were interviewed to get their views on the current serving Women Pastors in the CCAP Zambia. Of the 27, one was a woman past Synod executive member. The data shows that 9 out of 27 pastors and elders have common views. They say that they do not have any problems with women being elected to high positions in the church. They make reference to Old and New Testament women who were used by God. The foregoing view makes them comfortable to state that women should be allowed to preach the word of God in the church because God has bestowed different spiritual gifts on men as well as on women. They argue that if God, in his infinite wisdom, did not plan that women should participate in the gospel proclamation, He would not have wasted his time to give women his spiritual gifts.

They argue that Paul did not make a universal cross-cutting injunction on women because he was addressing problems that he encountered in Corinth and Ephesus. They agree that most members do not understand the texts under study. They assume that the reason for this is our cultural differences on women which dictate our interpretation of the passages.

They argued that female ministers could appropriately hold all key positions in the Synod assuming the person is well grounded theologically. In fact, women are theologically trained in the same way as men. So, it is not possible to limit the role of women to one or the other position. They argued that women too have potential leadership qualities that need to be utilized because women pay attention to detail

---

[65] A sampling of 27 Synod leader's past and present in total in Zambia was conducted. 13 were all male pastors dotted across the country. At the time of this study, the clergy ministered in Lundazi, Lusaka and Ndola. The other 14 were elders. Out of the 14, only one was female. At the time of this study, these elders worked in Southern, Lusaka, Copperbelt and Eastern Provinces of Zambia.

and like to make follow-up. Also, because these women are called, they too are children of God through faith, and God calls His children to lead His Church regardless of gender, for the New Testament—particularly Paul's letter to the Galatians 3:26-29—advocates equality in Christ. They argued that in Christ there is no male and female; hence women too are eligible for any office when serving Jesus Christ. They observed that women contributed much to the ministry of Jesus and the church after Jesus' crucifixion. They further argued that both men and women need organizational skills, servant leadership skills, knowledge of church polity and knowledge of history of the denomination.

However, they observed that a woman in a key position of the church would need to understand that she will encounter resistance and opposition, especially from other women; therefore, she needs to be focused, depend on God, and have the support of her spouse and the church at large. They argued that both women and men have different strengths and weaknesses. They went on to argue that a woman with strong organizational skills and constructive vision, that is, ability to plan, delegate, supervise, communicate in a positive way would make a good General Secretary as is also needed in the case of a man. Also, a woman with a pastoral caring attitude with a strong understanding of church polity would make a good Moderator.[66]

Eighteen (both clergy and elders) say that they have a problem with putting women in some high positions like that of a church pastor, Moderator or General Secretary. Though women have spiritual gifts like men, men cannot take their message preached from pulpits seriously.[67] These leaders have also shown that they are not conversant with the position of the church on women. Many argued that female ministers could not be in key church positions due to economic challenges and that the synod is still at a developing stage. They argued that voting in

---

[66] These were the 9 out of the 27 Synod leaders interviewed.

[67] These were the 18 out of the 27 Synod leaders interviewed.

female ministers would be like just punishing them. The Synod office currently faces serious economic challenges and putting female ministers could be a stumbling block for the church to move forward. Women have more needs than men. However, women should wait until such a time that the church has enough resources to run the Synod offices before they can be Executive members, Coordinators of Guilds and Departments.[68] This argument appears to me to indicate that women are not restricted to hold positions in the church. But this argument is misplaced because already female ministers are coping well in their respective presbyteries and congregations. In fact, some women are said to be doing fine in those congregations where male ministers have failed. If female ministers are capable of mobilizing both human and economic resources, how would they fail to use the same skill when they are in key Synod positions? They argued that women are short tempered, are poor public speakers and are unable to maintain confidentiality when they are provoked. Because of these facts women cannot make good leaders.[69] These arguments can only be sustained if male leaders are able to control their temperaments and keep confidentiality.

Women Laity Leaders' Responses

A total of 38 Congregation, Presbytery and Synod Christian Women Guild leaders past and present[70] throughout the country were interviewed to get their views on the current serving Women Pastors in the CCAP Zambia in relation to the passages under study among whom

---

[68] Ibid.

[69] Ibid.

[70] A sampling of 38 congregations, presbyteries and Synod Christian Women Guild Leaders were interviewed during their National Conference in Chipata from 25 to 30 August, 2015. However, of the 38 only 23 came and the other 15 were interviewed in their homes in Lusaka, Copperbelt, Southern, Eastern and Muchinga provinces.

was one first Synod Christian Women Guild coordinator. The data shows that 35% of the respondents have common views. They say that they do not have any problems with women being elected to high positions in the church.

Women too are capable, but they have to prove it. Men and women are different. They have different roles, so if a woman wants to take a role that does not belong to her naturally she has to work extra hard to prove that she can do it. Nature makes men and women different, but these differences do not add up to female inferiority or male superiority. Women can make very good ministers and leaders, but the issue is calling and working in panic. These respondents indicated that females would make better ministers because they are motherly, they have good negotiating skills, and since women have many problems, and the large membership of the church are women, they will be able to assist them and the women will be very free. Women are perceived to be more understanding, to be good stewards and as being more gifted than men.

But some of their performance is hindered by male church elders who feel that women cannot rule them. In addition, the female folk also are not supportive of their fellow women ministers. Usually people receive women ministers with hesitation as to whether they will make it or not, so women have to prove that they can perform. Some are of the opinion that men are easily accepted even if they are non-performers, but people find it difficult to accept women even if they are star performers.

In terms of respect, 65% of the people interviewed indicated that women ministers are not respected in the same way as male ministers. There are very few members in congregations that respect female ministers. Equality between men and women is only in being created in God's image and not in sharing leadership positions.

The Performance of Female Ministers

The female ministers in CCAP Zambia are all good preachers. They are currently performing well in terms of ministry and they need encouragement from male ministers, because they complement them and vice versa.[71] They observed that in some congregations where male ministers had failed to perform, female ministers have performed very well, especially Rev Kondwani Nkhoma of Kalulushi and Susan Nyirenda of Luanshya congregations. They have managed to organize Christians to build manses and the congregations have grown.[72] However, others argued that many of them lack effective relational and communication skills. They are not strong in pastoral care and visitation. They tend to be confrontational and defensive with both men and women congregants. They want to exert their authority as female ministers to show their weight. They tend to look down on others and some female ministers have tried to betray even their own husbands to leadership.[73] However, both male and female Ministers would benefit from additional training in pastoral counselling, administration, management, communication and organizational skills.[74]

Challenges Female Ministers Face

It has already been pointed out that the issue of ordination of female ministers is a new social-cultural paradigm in the church. In as far as the church appreciates the positive role of the services of female ministers; this research reveals some challenges.

Most of the people interviewed cited that women become busy with home business. Owing to their physiological nature, the women may at

---

[71] These were the 9 out of the 27 Synod leaders interviewed and 23 respondents of the 38 Christian women guilds interviewed.

[72] Ibid.

[73] Information from 18 respondents of the 27 synod leaders interviewed.

[74] These were the 9 out of the 27 Synod leaders interviewed

one point become pregnant and there may be need for them to go on maternity leave.[75] One informant said the major challenge is that the woman carries the baby in her womb for close to nine months and that during that time she would not be in a position to carry out her duties.[76] Others argued that women who desire to join the Holy Ministry have to make important decisions concerning family. One of them could be whether it would be convenient for them to have children, remain single or marry.[77]

It is difficult for a single female minister to find marriage. Some respondents said that when one becomes a minister, people treat the office with high esteem. Men feel intimidated to fall in love with a woman minister. Theology makes people courageous. This implies that the woman may remain single while the parents want to see grandchildren. They are fearful daughters and will not marry.[78] Also, the parents are not very sure whether their daughters would complete training without becoming pregnant in college. This in turn would bring shame on the entire clan.[79]

People's mind-set has not changed concerning women. Most people look down upon women ministers since they are not used to women's ministry.[80] Others argued that male ministers think that they cannot be equals with women ministers. They can't be colleagues because, traditionally, women are considered to be inferior to men. It is difficult

---

[75] Information from 18 respondents of the 27 synod leaders interviewed and the 23 respondents out of the 38 Christian women guild members sampled.

[76] This informant comes from Lundazi Presbytery, a woman among the sampled respondents preferred to be called JP.

[77] Information from 18 respondents of the 27 synod leaders interviewed.

[78] Ibid.

[79] Ibid.

[80] Information from the 23 respondents of the 38 Christian women guild members interviewed.

to accept that men and women are equal.[81] One female minister mentioned that even being a Presbytery Moderator or Clerk is frowned upon by men and women. People want to see whether women are credible and responsible. Women have to prove that they can really do it and this is quite stressful for women.[82] Centralized church structures have tended to oppress women in churches by denying them provision to engage themselves in spiritual ministries they feel called to.[83] Although female ministers have enjoyed and appreciated leadership in presbyteries and over fellow women, they are not satisfied with such a role. Women desire also to be in key leadership positions in CCAP Zambia.[84]

Transportation can be a challenge for women if they are posted to remote areas. One female minister explained that as the first minister she had to cycle fifty to seventy kilometers to get to some places. This can pose a challenge for some women who may not be as strong as men.[85] Some argued that this kind of thinking makes women look at Holy Ministry as suitable only for men who can be transferred anywhere and anytime.[86] Even though this is the age of motorbikes or vehicles, very few if any can afford to buy them. Most congregations in remote areas are very poor and can hardly afford a bicycle.[87]

One role of a minister is to do visitations with the session clerk. A challenge comes in because in most congregations, the session clerks

---

[81] Ibid.

[82] Int. Rev T.T. Chipeta, Chitala CCAP Congregation, Lundazi, 21.5.2015.

[83] Information from 18 respondents of the 27 synod leaders interviewed.

[84] Information from 9 respondents of the 27 synod leaders interviewed.

[85] Int. Rev Kondwani Nkhoma, Kalulushi CCAP Congregation, Kitwe, 24.5.2015.

[86] Information from 18 respondents of the 27 synod leaders interviewed.

[87] Information from 9 respondents of the 27 synod leaders interviewed.

are men, one of the problems that a woman pastor may face is that if the session clerk is male, she may find it difficult to visit Christians together with him. This brings suspicions and creates character assassinations.[88] The Synod has not yet put a policy encouraging congregations to have a woman session clerk if the minister is female. The position of session clerk is considered a male position.[89] Some informants cited Emusa CCAP congregation, no woman has occupied the post of session clerk since 1910, when the church was established, despite the fact that women have been elders for ages.[90] They contended that this still is a phenomenon in most CCAP congregations that only men hold this position of session clerk.[91]

The other challenge is the posting of ministers married to fellow ministers. As much as the church appreciates the positive role of the services of married couples who are both ministers; the trend has brought challenges both to the church and to these very couples.[92] The current church polity demands that each student who has been trained as a minister is posted to his or her congregation where he or she serves as parish minister.[93] How then should those ministers who marry fellow ministers be posted since they cannot serve in the same congregation? This gives us a picture of how much the church struggles to post those married couples who are both ministers, as most congregations are far apart, especially in the rural areas. The church has problems to find two

---

[88] Ibid.

[89] Ibid.

[90] This was confirmed by the researcher by talking to some long serving elders and Ministers. Also, the person cited confirmed that he had been Session Clerk for 32 years. His name is Josiah Shonga of Emusa CCAP Congregation.

[91] These informants came from Chasefu, Chasefu South, Lundazi presbyteries of the 38 sampled respondents.

[92] Information from 18 respondents of the 27 synod leaders interviewed.

[93] Ibid.

congregations that are near enough to each other where these couples can serve.[94]

In the same vein, the church finds it very difficult to transfer ministers married to each other, so that the Staffing Committee really struggles to transfer these couples.[95] Transfers of ministers are done due to the fact that ministers are not called to serve at one congregation on a permanent basis. At times, ministers may be rejected by their congregations for failure to perform their duties effectively or due to misconduct or prejudice. Transferring such ministers becomes a problem for the church because there are few open congregations that can take such couples.[96] The issue of posting and transfers of ministers is not only a challenge to the church leadership but also to the couples themselves. The church leadership of the CCAP does not consider the issue of distance between the two congregations where the married ministers may be serving, when posting and making transfers.[97] For example, Rev MacDonald Nyirenda serves in Kwacha CCAP Congregation in another presbytery and stays with the wife at Luanshya CCAP congregation. This makes mobility difficult and expensive for the spouse staying at the manse of the congregation of the spouse.[98] One married female minister pointed out that the service of the minister, who may be staying at the spouse's manse, becomes very bad, because of the

---

[94] Information from 9 respondents of the 27 synod leaders interviewed.

[95] Int. Rev M.R. Kabandama, General Secretary, Synod Offices, Lusaka, 18.5.2015.

[96] Int. Rev C.T. Soko, Synod Executive Member, Matero CCAP Congregation, Lusaka, 9.7.2015.

[97] Information from 9 respondents of the 27 synod leaders interviewed.

[98] Int. Rev M.R. Kabandama, General Secretary, Synod Offices, Lusaka, 18.5.2015.

travelling involved. She said that it is even worse in cases where the congregation is not financially sound.⁹⁹

Also, the maintenance of the family bonds between the two is affected.¹⁰⁰ It is impossible to think that these ministers should live in their respective congregations because they are resident ministers.¹⁰¹ An executive member explained that the CCAP values the family very much, but the problem it is encountering is failure to maintain the family bonds of those ministers who marry fellow ministers. That may lead to unfaithfulness. Married couples must not live separately because they are parish ministers. Since some people have a negative attitude towards female ministers, it is even worse to accept them in their congregations when they realize that she is married to a fellow minister. This arises due to the fact that married couples have to stay away from each other for weeks as they discharge parish duties.¹⁰² But others argued that it was senseless to begin to think that the church should stop ordaining female ministers or stop those who fall in love with fellow ministers from marrying each other. This is because no one can limit love or God's calling for people.¹⁰³

Factors Limiting Women's Participation in Holy Ministry

Culture

Seventy-six percent of the people interviewed cited tradition as one of the major factors that inhibit women from applying for the holy ministry. Women are not applying because they feel out of place since

---

⁹⁹ This Female Minister preferred to be called madam S.B.

¹⁰⁰ Information from 18 respondents of the 27 synod leaders interviewed.

¹⁰¹ Ibid.

¹⁰² This Executive member of the Synod preferred to be called Mr XY.

¹⁰³ Information from 9 respondents of the 27 synod leaders interviewed.

they are not supported by their culture.[104] When a woman ventures into the office of the minister, she is frowned upon and some women feel uncomfortable with that. Both men and women are not used to women in Holy Ministry. People are still conservative due to cultural ideologies where women are not expected to have authority over men. Due to this patriarchy, males dominate the social hierarchy and inheritance is often traced through the male line. The male role gives men more power and socializes them towards the attainment of power while females are socialized in such a way that they submit to the male power. Men have often monopolized power in Church. This is the accepted norm.[105]

However, in matrilineal societies in Zambia, women have been leaders such as spirit mediums and chiefs.[106] On another level, traditional matrilineal culture has been applauded by many scholars for elevating women's engagement in society, and this has raised the concern that these women do not always have such freedoms in their church.[107] It would be wrong therefore to suggest that women could not be leaders because traditionally they cannot speak in public. It is not clear whether CCAP Zambia women get this stand from the Bible or from their culture; although there may be a possibility that some may use the Levitical passagees to cement the view.[108]

Some of the patriarchal oppression in culture that women deal with is related to one's identity, belonging, marriage stability and religious

---

[104] Information from 18 respondents of the 27 synod leaders interviewed.

[105] Ibid.

[106] Isabel Phiri, *Women, Presbyterianism and Patriarchy*, Blantyre: CLAIM-Kachere, 2000, pp. 32-34.

[107] Rachel NyaGondwe Banda [Fiedler], *Women of the Bible and Culture*, Zomba: Kachere, 2005, p. 191.

[108] Int. Rev David Chiboboka, CTC Principal and former General Secretary CCAP Zambia, Lundazi, 15.5.2015.

misconceptions about women.[109] It indeed requires multiple interpretative tools to unsettle these culture related patriarchal oppressions. As the women engage in this game of reinterpreting culture, they grapple with the old issues of continuity and discontinuity of cultural elements in the light of what is liberating and what is not. While this is easy for some African women, for others it is a nightmare goal to achieve because of conflictual realities in their lives which present a change in making choices on what is liberating and what is not. The change is slow among women in a patriarchal context, likely because the low position of women in the church was cemented not only by missionary Christianity, but also by their traditional culture.[110]

Lack of Confidence

Seventy-nine of the men and women interviewed indicated that women are not authoritative enough and as such they cannot make good ministers. Most of them are shy and they doubt their abilities. Women as ministers are therefore given less respect because they lack the rank of masculinity that people expect to see in them.[111] Such restrictions are based on cultural beliefs and biblical interpretations or a lack of self-confidence.[112] What lacks in women is courage; they seem to be full of fear and there is that feeling that they cannot manage the challenge of running a congregation. In other words, they lack confidence. Women suffer from an inferiority complex.[113] Public speaking is seen as a challenge for many women but they do not know that the training at

---

[109] Information from the 23 Women Guild leaders who attended their Synodical conference in Chipata.

[110] Rachel NyaGondwe Banda [Fiedler], *Women of Bible and Culture*, Zomba: Kachere, 2005, p. 191.

[111] Information from 18 of the 27 synod leaders interviewed and from 23 of the 38 women interviewed.

[112] Ibid.

[113] Information 18 respondents of the 27 synod leaders interviewed.

the theological college will prepare them in this area as well. They would benefit from additional training in communication skills.[114]

This is also seen as true when it comes to Kirk sessions, Presbytery, Synod or even Vestry meetings; female church elders contribute very little during deliberations because they are not confident that they will say something sensible. Women elders do participate in the sessions, even though their participation is minimal. Women rarely speak during sessions due to timidity.[115] Even though women have been entrusted with leadership positions, they do not make maximum use of the opportunity. When they are put on the spot to say something on a particular issue, they usually demonstrate submissiveness to what men have already said. They have low self-esteem and seem to have the fear of the unknown. It is believed that what men say should be taken wholesale and should not be challenged. In many instances, there are very few women who are bold enough to speak. For this reason, few women are expected to speak each time the session convenes.[116] Although women are many, most Church positions are held by men in CCAP Zambia.[117]

Another view is that women are not convinced that they can be leaders because they are not courageous in the face of challenges. They give up quickly, unlike men, and they are busy people. The respondents argued that it is somehow difficult for them to leave the home.[118] Churches, which have a history of women playing subservient roles, have

---

[114] Information from 9 respondents of the 27 synod leaders interviewed.

[115] Int. Rev L.M. Nyirenda, Retired Synod Moderator, Mphamba CCAP Congregation, Lundazi, 10.6.2015.

[116] Information from 18 respondents of the 27 synod leaders interviewed and from 23 of the 38 women interviewed.

[117] Ibid.

[118] Ibid.

impacted women negatively to such an extent that some of them have started believing that women ought not to be leaders.[119]

Lack of Academic Qualification

Although there is a steady rise of women studying theology in CCAP Zambia, there has been low enrolment of women since the Synod accepted ordination of women to Holy Ministry. The General Secretary pointed out the problem of low enrolment of female students, among other factors, low literacy levels of women and lack of opportunities to utilize theological training in churches.[120] Most females who have a calling to ministry, as recorded in the Synod minutes, do not meet the required qualifications. They were asked to re-write or upgrade their academic qualifications, which they have not done, hence they fall out. In other words, qualifications act as a barrier for some women. The entry qualification is Zambia School Certificate of Education with at least four credits including English.[121] Some women may be called by God but they may not have the necessary qualifications and this discourages them.[122] Three presbyteries observed that, with the new development in the Synod of admitting female candidates to the Holy Ministry, the Synod should review admission conditions as an affirmative action to promote the participation of women in the Holy Ministry. This might increase the enrolment levels and create equal participation in decision making positions in the church as is the current practice of the Government of Zambia on gender equality.[123]

---

[119] Information from 9 respondents of the 27 synod leaders interviewed.

[120] Int. Rev M.R. Kabandama, General Secretary, Lusaka, 13.8.2015.

[121] Ibid, 13.8.2015.

[122] Information from the 23 Christian women Guild leaders who attended their Synodical conference in Chipeta.

[123] The three presbyteries include: Chasefu, Lundazi and Midlands from where some respondents of the 38 Christian women Guild leaders came.

"Women are Easily Tempted"

Eighty percent of the respondents said that women cannot make good ministers because they are easily tempted. Both women and men felt that women are weak and can easily be tempted because they move with fashion.[124] Some women said that there are a lot of rules for ministers and as such women ministers will not be free. They may not be comfortable to decorate themselves as this may make them look like they belong to 'the world.' They said that it is very difficult for women to make it in Holy Ministry because they covet a lot of things. They want the best of everything, so they can easily be tricked.[125] A common example is how the story of Eve is presented against woman's empowerment. The story is used to argue that because Eve is the one who gave the forbidden fruit to Adam, she made Adam sin. This biblical reflection is taken as a reason why in some churches women cannot be ordained as pastors or apply to be ordained.[126] Some cited the many pregnancies and girls' dropping out from school as evidence of the statement that women are easily tempted.[127] But others said this argument can only be sustained if the men and boys who tempt stop coaxing the girls. It is true that the Bible presents Eve as the one who sinned first, but this is no justification for stopping women from joining Holy Ministry, because the same Bible states that men and women are equally sinners (Romans 3:23).[128] The other story is that of a woman caught in adultery where Jesus asks those around to throw a stone at

---

[124] Information from 18 respondents of the 27 synod leaders interviewed and from 23 of the 38 women interviewed.

[125] Information from the 23 Christian women Guild leaders who attended their Synodical conference in Chipata.

[126] Rachel NyaGondwe Fiedler, "The Circle of Concerned African Women Theologians (1989-2007): History and Theology," PhD, University of the Free State, 2010, p. 85.

[127] Information from 18 respondents of the 27 synod leaders interviewed.

[128] Information from 9 respondents of the 27 synod leaders interviewed.

her if they did not sin. Here the people expose the sin of the woman and hide that of the man that is later exposed by Jesus.[129]

Holy Ministry has Poor Conditions of Service

The majority of the people interviewed maintained that ministers get very low pay and as such ministry is not attractive to many women. There is no enjoyment in Holy Ministry because there are few privileges. In most cases relatives discourage girls because parents educate children so that they can in turn help them as well as their siblings. It appears that conditions are worse for ministers who stay in remote places. So those who have expressed interest to become ministers have gone back on their decisions because of that.[130] It is important to note that it is not only females who are faced with the challenge of low pay, but males as well.[131] Other women may not be bold enough to go into Holy Ministry until they see whether the women ministers are prospering in terms of positions and material and financial aspects. Several women will be attracted when they see women ministers prospering.[132] This, however, goes against the requirement that a person who joins Holy Ministry must do so out of divine calling. What this idea implies is that one would obey God only when she sees that there is prosperity. It is not strange to see some people joining Holy Ministry for reasons other than calling and such things cannot be ruled

---

[129] Rachel NyaGondwe Fiedler, "The Circle of Concerned African Women Theologians (1989-2007): History and Theology," PhD, University of the Free State, 2010, p. 85.

[130] Information from 18 respondents of the 27 synod leaders interviewed and from 23 of the 38 women interviewed.

[131] Information from 18 respondents of the 27 synod leaders interviewed.

[132] Information from 18 respondents of the 27 synod leaders interviewed and from 23 of the 38 women interviewed.

out.[133] Others argued that some people have joined Holy Ministry because they had nothing to do but they would not openly say so.[134]

"The Models have Failed"

Seventy-eight percent of the people interviewed indicated that family issues are one of the main factors that lead to few applications of women to Holy Ministry. This issue is connected to that of finding life partners. The conception is that almost all the ladies who are in Holy Ministry or were in the process of becoming ministers appear to have failed on issues to do with marriage.[135] These are women who went for theological training while single. It must be clear that getting married to people from other Christian denominations is acceptable, but it may not be convenient for women in Holy Ministry.[136] Many women argued that some women are only interested to use theological education for their personal gain as they refuse to be ordained as ministers, yet the church spends money on them.[137] This in itself closes doors for others who genuinely want to serve God but partners may not be ready to find more scholarships. Also, many of them lack effective relational and communication skills. They tend to be confrontational and defensive with both men and women congregants. They want to exert their authority as pastors to show their weight.[138] Others argued that most

---

[133] Information from the 23 Christian women Guild leaders who attended their Synodical conference in Chipata.

[134] Information from 18 respondents of the 27 synod leaders interviewed and 23 of the 38 women interviewed.

[135] Ibid.

[136] Information from 18 respondents of the 27 synod leaders interviewed.

[137] Information from the 23 Christian women Guild leaders who attended their Synodical conference in Chipata.

[138] Ibid.

female ministers feel they are more important than fellow lay women they are leading and as such they cannot take constructive criticism.[139]

Conclusion

This chapter reveals that in CCAP Zambia provision of space for women leadership still remains a challenge. The battle for women's ordination was a long process and the women finally won. There are still women who are bound by tradition and feel that men should lead in all areas. The women themselves are not supportive of each other giving enough evidence that only men can be leaders. This is clear in the views of those in leadership, women in theology and women laity that women are passive beings. What became clear in my study was that in some cases all three groups of participants: Synod leaders, women pastors, and the women laity leaders, had similar expectations about the role of the women in CCAP Zambia. In other expressed cases, there were conflicting expectations among all three groups of participants on what should be the roles of the women, which led to some tension. Also, there is difference in understanding of the provision of space for women leadership. It is this patriarchal form of church, with its all-male clerical control as well as its authoritarian and hierarchical structures, which feminist ecclesiology challenges. This continues to be oppressive towards women by ruling over and excluding them from full participation in ministry.[140] All forms of oppressive language used to describe women, including texts which oppress and marginalize women and exclude them from all essential processes of representation and self-definition still seem to be a challenge.

---

[139] Information from 18 respondents of the 27 synod leaders interviewed and 23 of the 38 women interviewed.

[140] Mary C Hilker, "Experience and Traditions: Can the Centre Hold?" In Catherine Milacugna (ed), *Freeing Theology: The Essentials of Theology in Feminist Perspective,* New York: Harper San Francisco, 1993, p. 76.

This chapter also reveals that most CCAP leaders appreciate the role of women as legally binding but the praxis suggests otherwise. On the one hand, the Synod leadership demonstrates acceptability; on the other hand, there is no practicality as regards to the views expressed towards that legality. One is tempted to suggest that the journey towards equality in CCAP Zambia is a pipe dream. Owanikin rightly observes that while women in society are increasingly holding leadership positions, the church still lags behind, resiliently holding on to its long-held traditions.[141] As noted by Isabel Phiri, it is the desire of women theologians that both women and men receive a relevant theological education that promotes female and male humanity as reflecting the image of God.[142] Phiri goes on to argue that

> such an education will help demystify the Bible so that it does not add to the oppression of women, but rather becomes life-giving as women understand God for themselves, instead of through an all-male pastor.[143]

The onus is on both women and those in leadership if the situation is to change for the better. Hence, as with culture, the Bible is a double-edged sword and it should be used with a hermeneutic of suspicion.[144]

---

[141] Owanikin R. Modupe, "The Priesthood of Church Women in the Nigerian Context," in Mercy Amba Oduyoye and Musimbi R. Kanyoro, *Will to Arise: Women, Tradition and the Church in Africa,* Pietermaritzburg: Cluster Publications, 2006, pp. 206-219.

[142] Isabel Apawo Phiri, "The Church as a Healing Community: Voices and Visions from Chilobwe Healing Centre," Isabel Apawo Phiri and Sarojini Nadar, *On Being Church: African Women's Voices and Visions,* Genève: World Council of Churches, 2005, pp. 29-46, esp. p. 34.

[143] Ibid, p. 34.

[144] Mercy Amba Oduyoye, *Introducing African Women's Theology,* Sheffield Academic Press, 2001, pp. 11-12. – Oduyoye and other Circle theologians use the image of the double edged sword, ascribing to it a healing and a destroying side, while in biblical imagery both sides of the sword are equally destroying (Heb 5:12, Prov 54, Ps 149:6).

For Oduyoye, the biblical narratives are embedded in multicultural layers, and cultural hermeneutics should enable women to view the Bible through African women's eyes and to extract from it what is liberating and life giving,[145] and Teresa Okure points out that although the creation account in the book of Genesis and the writings of Paul have been misinterpreted to determine the role and status of women in church and society, there is a liberative side of the story and other biblical stories where women are shown as God's co-workers and agents of life, apart from being mothers.[146]

---

[145] Ibid, p. 12.

[146] Teresa Okure, in *Women in the Bible with Passion and Compassion: Third World Women Doing Theology,* Virginia Fabella and Mercy Amba Oduyoye (eds), Maryknoll: Orbis, 1988, pp. 47-59 [52].

Chapter 3

The Place of Women in the Greco-Roman World

Introduction

This chapter provides an analysis of the place of Women in the Greco-Roman World. It looks at the situation of women in Greek, Roman and Jewish cultures of the time as a background to understand the place of women in the Pauline Texts.

Women in Ancient Greek Culture

Strict gender roles and standards of conduct governed the lives of Greek women. Autonomy, control and overall freedom were considered the realm of men who were free to come and go, who played an active role in public life, and who controlled and restricted the life of women.[1]

In Ancient Greek society male citizens were divided into the *aristoi*- landed aristocrats, *periokoi*- less wealthy farmers, and middle class artisans and traders newly wealthy but without land who were unable to rise to positions of power. Below them were the semi-free laborers, the slaves (*douloi*), and foreigners (*xenoi* and *metoicoi*).[2]

Female citizens (with the exception of Spartan women) were unable to vote, own land or inherit. Those whose husbands belonged to the *aristoi* and *periokoi* remained in the home, raising children and engaging in wool work, weaving and other indoor activities. Respectable women lived in a women's quarter (gynaeceum) from where they ran the home

---

[1] Amanda Evans, "Women in the Greek and Roman Perspective," 2003, http://housatonic.net/faculty/ABALL/PrimarySourceDocs/168.htm, [16.8.2016].

[2] Mark Cartwright, Women in ancient Greece", 2018, www.ancient.eu/article/907/women-in-ancient Greece.

and distanced themselves from contact with men.³ Women did not join their husbands when they entertained guests, they were not allowed to speak in public and it was considered inappropriate for them to discuss or argue with their husbands in private.⁴ They were expected to be obedient in all things their husbands required of them.⁵ Yet women did go out of the home to attend festivals and funerals. It is probable, but not certain, that they were able to go to the theater.⁶

Women below the landed classes were divided according to a moral standard that separated women in respectable positions from those in disgraceful professions, and separated women labourers from slaves. Women were also ranked based on age and marital status including young virgin, celibate adult, wife, or widow.⁷

The sixth-century law code of Solon legalized prostitution in Athens, and women served as brothel prostitutes (*porne*) or as higher class prostitutes (*hetaera*) trained in music and culture.⁸ Greek women also had a religious role. The woman priest of Athena Polias, the patron goddess of Athens, was important and influential in the political life of Athens in the Classical and Hellenistic periods which extended from 500-146 BC. On the annual feast of the Panathenaea, women and men participated in the processions and young virgins carried baskets. When

---

[3] N. Bamanie, "Women in Ancient Greece," 2016, p. 1, www.researchgate.net/profile/Nuray_Bamanie.

[4] Amanda Evans, "Women in the Greek and Roman Perspective," 2003, p. 4, http://housatonic.net/faculty/Aball/PrimarySourceDocs/168.htm,[16.8. 2016]

[5] Ibid.

[6] Elizabeth M. Tetlow, "The Status of Women in Greek, Roman and Jewish Society," 1980, p. 4, www.womenpriests.org/classic/tetlow1.asp, [20.6.2017].

[7] Laura Stempmorlok, "1 Timothy 2:9,10: Greco - Roman Women," http://thirdwaystyle.wordpress.com/author/laurastempmorlok [15.5.2015].

[8] Mark Cartwright, "Ancient Greek Society," 2018, p. 2, www.ancient.eu/-article /483/ancient-greek-society.

syncretistic mystery cults became prominent in the empire during the Hellenistic period (420-146 BC), women exercised a leadership role and many women converted to them. Some women priests were married, others lived in celibate communities. Women priests and religious functionnaries were publicly honoured in Hellenistic society.[9]

The primary duty of women in ancient Athens was to marry and to continue the family unit by bearing legitimate children. A daughter who inherited property when there was no son, was required to marry her next of kin. At marriage a dowry was given and it was maintained so the wife might receive eighteen percent interest on it annually for her support. By law either partner might initiate divorce, but the wife, who had to be aided in the procedure by her father, seldom filed for divorce. The children, considered the property of the husband, remained with him in cases of divorce.[10]

Marriages in Athens during the classical period (500-420 BC) were arranged by parents. A girl was expected to marry by the time she was fourteen. She had only a few years for her education, which took place in the home and was primarily focused on domestic affairs. Educated women were thought to be dangerous to men.[11]

Plato (428-327 BC), the famous Athenian philosopher of the classical period, developed a concept of equality for women in his book *The Republic* which defined an ideal city-state. In the book Plato argued with his companion Glaucon as follows:

---

[9] Elizabeth M. Tetlow, "The Status of Women in Greek, Roman and Jewish Society," 1980, p. 7, www.womenpriests.org/classic/tetlow1.asp, [20.6.2017].

[10] www.GreekBoston.com [18.8.20].

[11] Elizabeth M. Tetlow, "The Status of Women in Greek, Roman and Jewish Society," 1980, p. 4, www.womenpriests.org/classic/tetlow1.asp, [20.6.2017].

> Men and women alike possess the qualities which make a guardian; they differ only in their comparative strength or weakness.
>
> Obviously.
>
> And those women who have such qualities are to be selected as the companions and colleagues of men who have similar qualities and whom they resemble in capacity and in character?
>
> Very true.
>
> And ought not the same natures to have the same pursuits?
>
> They ought.
>
> Then, as we were saying before, there is nothing unnatural in assigning music and gymnastic to the wives of the guardians—to that point we come round again.
>
> Certainly not.[12]

According to Plato's writings, women were to be allowed great freedom and the right to participate in politics. Women were to be educated for the good of the state and trained to fight to defend the state. As guardians, competent women would rule over both men and women. Yet even in the *Republic*, Plato indicated that the place of woman was within the confines of her home.[13]

Plato's student Aristotle argued that men and women are unequal by nature.

> The temperance of a man and of a woman or the courage and justice of a man and of a woman are not, as Socrates maintained, the same. The courage of a man is shown in commanding and of a woman in obeying ... as the poet says of women "silence is a woman's glory" but this is not equally the glory of man.[14]

---

[12] Plato, *The Republic,* p. 316.

[13] Elizabeth M. Tetlow, "The Status of Women in Greek, Roman and Jewish Society," 1980, p. 4, www.womenpriests.org/classic/tetlow1.asp, [20.6.2017]

[14] Aristotle, *Politics,* p. 24.

Aristotle considered man superior and woman inferior. Wives and daughters were destined to obey their husbands and fathers. The role of women was obedience and silence. Tetlow suggests that the general social practice and mores of Athens during the classical period were based on Aristotle's writings.[15]

Tetlow indicates that women were not completely secluded in the classical period in Athens, although many men preferred that they would be. Social and political freedom was limited; however some women sought a role and a voice in their society.[16] Athenian women were permitted to testify in court, were generally literate and had some understanding of economics and politics. It is unlikely that all women complied with the cultural ideal of seclusion and silence.[17]

The *Moralia* of Plutarch, written in the first century AD, described the behaviours and morals of the ancient Greeks. He noted that in marriage it was said that all land belonged to the husband even if the wife contributed the larger part of the estate. Wives were to be seen only in the company of their husbands. Plutarch believed that an education in philosophy, literature, geometry and astronomy benefitted women and that the husband might serve as his wife's teacher. As a result the pair would enjoy a more interesting life together. When husband and wife disagreed, Plutarch encouraged men to persuade their wives through the use of reason, rather than force.[18]

---

[15] Elizabeth M. Tetlow, "The Status of Women in Greek, Roman and Jewish Society," 1980, p. 4, www.womenpriests.org/classic/tetlow1.asp, [20.6.2017].

[16] Ibid, p. 3.

[17] Ibid, pp. 5-29.

[18] Elizabeth M. Tetlow, "The Status of Women in Greek, Roman and Jewish Society," 1980, p. 5, www.womenpriests.org/classic/tetlow1.asp, [20.6.2017]

Tetlow discusses the place of Greek women in the Hellenistic period in Greece (420-146 BC).[19] She argues that during the Hellenistic period the position and role of women within society changed because society as a whole faced many challenges and changes. Through the conquests of Alexander the Great (356-323 BC), a great military strategist, city states were supplanted by an immense empire. The Greek, Syrian and Egyptian queens of the time held real political power. Women in general within the empire began to learn how to protect themselves since they were without the kind of male protection they had in Greece. Through personal wealth women gained economic power which enabled them to obtain legal rights and a voice in public affairs. Some were recognized for their generous support of the State. Hellenistic marriage contracts stated various different rights and obligations for both spouses. In the case of divorce, the wife was given back her dowry, and the husband continued to support the children. The husband retained communal property. Husbands could take concubines, and prostitution was legal.[20] Upper-class women received some degree of education and many were literate. Hipparchus, a woman philosopher among the Cynics, taught in public with her husband. Women became competent professionals in athletics, music, poetry, literature, philosophy, oratory, medicine and various crafts. Some women were equal in status to men politically and economically. Class barriers began to break down and the family institution was weakened.[21]

In contrast to the limited role of Athenian women during the Classical and Hellenistic periods of Greek history, women in the city-state of Sparta were allowed to own property, become citizens, and be

---

[19] Ibid. p 5
[20] Ibid. p 6
[21] Ibid. p 6

educated. To say that all Ancient Greek women were submissive is incorrect.[22]

According to Plutarch, a Spartan legislator named Lycurgus introduced to Sparta a unique social system and constitution focused on the virtues of equality, military fitness and austerity. Lycurgus placed maximum emphasis on military proficiency through physical development and military training; as a result Spartans excelled in battle, and Sparta rose to military dominance in ancient Greece around 650 BCE.[23] Spartan women were expected to exercise. Lycurgus

> ordered the maidens to exercise themselves with wrestling, running, throwing the quoit, and casting the dart, to the end that the fruit they conceived might, in strong and healthy bodies, take firmer root and find better growth, and withal that they, with this greater vigour, might be the more able to undergo the pains of child-bearing. And to the end he might take away their over great tenderness and fear of exposure to the air, and all acquired womanishness, he ordered that the young women should go naked in the processions, as well as the young men, and dance, too, in that condition, at certain solemn feasts..."[24]

The most important role of women in Sparta was the bearing of strong children, especially boys fit for military life.[25] In order to bear strong babies, women were to be fed equal rations, and to be educated and trained in athletics. Maternal mortality was less of a danger in Sparta

---

[22] M. Cartwright, "Women in Ancient Greece," www.ancient.eu/artiticle/ 927 /women-in-ancient Greece/2016.

[23] Robertson https://medium.com/stoicism-philosophy-as-a-way-of-life/the-spartan-philosophy-of-life-f0731afdb039

[24] Plutarch, *Lycurgus*: 75 AD, p 8.

[25] Ibid.

than in other city-states because Spartan women married at a later age.[26]

Toward the end of the period many women in Sparta had become quite wealthy and limited the population by refusing to bear many children. Spartan women were portrayed by Plutarch as heroic and proud.[27] In Sparta women had the right to own, control and inherit property. A certain percentage of what a woman produced through her work belonged to her. In divorce, a woman retained half her property. It is known that there were at least nine women poets during this period. A few are known by name, such as Corinna and Sappho, but little of their poetry has been preserved. These women were educated and belonged to the upper class of society. Thus, they enjoyed the freedom and the leisure to be able to write.[28]

In Sparta a family's land was shared between all members of the family. This included the girls although their percentage was smaller than that of their brothers. At the beginning of the classical period, a Spartan woman could inherit part of her family's estate but rather than owning it, she passed it on to her children. Towards the end of the classical period, Xenophon and Aristotle noted that, without a male's approval, women owned and managed, controlled, and disposed of property.[29]

Near the end of the classical period, Aristotle indicated that Spartan women owned two-fifths of the land. Because women owned significant land and because Spartan men were constantly away training or at war, the women were responsible for managing the household and

---

[26] Elizabeth M. Tetlow, "The Status of Women in Greek, Roman and Jewish Society," 1980, p. 3, www.womenpriests.org/classic/tetlow1.asp, [20.6.2017]

[27] Ibid, p. 3

[28] Ibid, p. 3.

[29] "The Role of Women in Spartan Society," https://phdessay.com/the-role-of-women-in-spartan-society-to-the-battle-of-leuctra-371-bc/ [12.4.2017].

the agricultural land. They supervised the servants who worked in the house and on land; they themselves did not perform domestic duties or manual labour.[30]

Women in Roman Culture

Roman Women had a very limited role in public life. They could not attend, speak in, or vote at political assemblies and they could not hold any position of political responsibility. Typical jobs undertaken by such women were in agriculture, markets, crafts, as midwives and as wet-nurses.[31] The status of Roman women was very low. Roman law placed a wife under the absolute control of her husband, who had ownership of her and all her possessions. He could divorce her if she went out in public without a veil. A husband had the power of life and death over his wife, just as he did over his children.[32] Roman law encouraged marriage for the sake of an orderly society with plentiful offspring whose parentage was unambiguous. Adultery was, therefore, seen primarily as a crime against the father of the woman, so that he was generally permitted to kill his daughter as well as the adulterer. The husband was also somewhat wronged and had a limited right to kill the adulterer, though not his wife.[33]

The Romans allowed marriages between closer family members than we would. It was permissible for first cousins to marry, and from the early empire on, uncles could even marry their nieces. Marriage was a political tool and used to cement an alliance between families or political factions. This desire to use children as political pawn led to children being engaged at very young ages, even sometimes as babies.

---

[30] Ibid.

[31] www.ancient.eu>article>th [29.8.2020].

[32] Svetlana Renee Papazov, "The Place of Women in the Graeco Roman World," p. 2, http://enrichment journal.ag.org, [15.8.2016].

[33] Ibid, p. 2.

To curb this, a law was passed stating that to be engaged, the two people had to be at least seven years old.[34]

Also, in the Roman World, women were culturally ranked according to several classes. The first class distinction was either that of Plebeians or of Patricians. Plebeians were people of lower class and Patricians were of higher class. From there women were divided according to a moral standard that separated respectable women from those in a disreputable profession, according to whether one is a slave or free, and by age.[35] Roman women lived in a world where strict gender roles were prescribed, where each person was judged in terms of compliance with gender-specific standards of conduct. Men were placed above women in terms of autonomy, control, and overall freedom. Men lived in the world at large, active in public life and free to come and go as they willed, but women's lives were sheltered. Women were assigned the role of homemaker, where they were expected to be good wives and mothers, but not much of anything else. A woman rarely achieved independence, being under the dominion of her father until he turned her over to her husband.[36]

But Roman women were not typically involved in politics, and few were taught to read or write. Many men viewed women as their inferiors, being subordinated and oppressed. However, women were also merchants, writers, philosophers, and even religious leaders. Women were not "cloistered in their homes" and contemporary Women's subordination was seen as a moral issue, as well as a legal and social one. It was important for a husband to govern his wife, because that

---

[34] https//www.thegreatcoursesdaily.com,(29.8.2020)

[35] Laura Stempmorlok, "1 Timothy 2:9, 10: Greco - Roman Women," http://thirdwaystyle.wordpress.com/author/laurastempmorlok [15.8.2016].

[36] Amanda Evans, "Women in the Greek and Roman Perspective," 2003, http://housatonic.net/faculty/aball/primarysourcedocs/168.htm, [16.8.2016].

marital relationship was the backbone of social stability.[37] However, by the first century AD women had much more freedom to manage their own business and financial affairs. Unless she had married in *manu*[38] a woman could own, inherit and dispose of property. By the time of Augustus, women with three children became legally independent, a status known as *'sui iuris.'* In reality, the degree of freedom a woman enjoyed depended largely on her wealth and social status.[39]

The status of women in the Roman Empire was influenced by the position of women in Hellenistic society. Women were allowed to participate independently in society and business. Many women possessed great wealth. Influenced by the example of Hellenistic queens who had also lived in an empire where their husbands were frequently absent on campaigns for long periods of time, Roman women began to exercise political power. Yet they rarely actually held political office. Women also influenced the men who held office through their economic power.[40]

Traditionally, sex roles were still accepted by Roman society. This fact created tension between the theoretical ideal of the woman staying at home and weaving, and the reality of historical women moving with relative freedom in the political arena and in the marketplace. Also, according to Roman law, women were under the complete control of the pater familias, the male head of the extended family unit. This power extended to life and death. A death penalty could be imposed

---

[37] Ibid.

[38] Manu means 'hand' in Latin, and this means a woman was regarded as piece of property that passed from the hand of the father to that of her husband.

[39] www.pbs.org>romans>women, [23.8.2017].

[40] Elizabeth M. Tetlow, "The Status of Women in Greek, Roman and Jewish Society," 1980, pp. 5-19, www.womenpriests.org/classic/tetlow1.asp, [20.6.2017].

upon a woman for adultery or drinking alcohol. The pater familias arranged marriages and appointed guardians for the women of his family. A woman could not legally transact business, make a contract or a will, or manumit a slave without the approval of her guardian. The law of guardians was not rigidly enforced and women frequently did transact business independently of them.[41] However wealthy they were, because they could not vote or stand for office, women had no formal role in public life. In reality, wives or close relatives of prominent men could have political influence behind the scenes and exert real, albeit informal, power. In public, though, women were expected to play their traditional role in the household. Women were expected to be the dignified wife and the good mother and, while these rules could be bent, they could not be broken. Julia, daughter to Emperor Augustus is a test case. Although she was renowned as a clever, vivacious woman with a sharp tongue, Augustus insisted that Julia spin and weave like plebeian women, to demonstrate her wifely virtues. He denounced her in public and banished her for the rest of her life. These were limits, even for an emperor's daughter.[42]

There were different types of marriage in Roman society. In *manus* marriage the woman left the control of the pater familias and came under the jurisdiction of her husband. This type of marriage tended to be more stable. In *non-manus* marriage the woman remained under the authority of her pater familias, which tended to give her more freedom.[43] Some women actually chose their own spouses. Most women married between the ages of twelve and fifteen. Divorce could be initiated by either spouse or by the wife's father. In subsequent marriages at a later age, women had greater choice in the selection of

---

[41] www.Pbs.org>romans>women, [18.8.2020]

[42] www.Pbs.org, [18.8.2020].

[43] Elizabeth M. Tetlow, "The Status of Women in Greek, Roman and Jewish Society", www.womenpriests.org/classic/tetlow1 (20.6.2017).

a spouse. This double standard was upheld by law. Only the adultery of a woman was a crime which required punishment.[44] Prostitution was legal. Marriages and divorces were arranged on the basis of political and economic reasons. Daughters were not given individual names. They were called by the feminine form of the name of their father.[45] Yet Roman women had a legal right to inherit. Some amassed great fortunes. The role of a wife was to manage the household. All chores were done by slaves, although the ideal wife was still expected to spin and weave like her ancient ancestors. The women of the upper classes were in reality free from work. They were able to go out: to market, to festivals, to attend banquets in mixed company. Status in Roman society was sought through public display of wealth. Some women in the imperial court were actually proclaimed gods in the state cult of emperor worship. Women were able to petition the Senate and even held protest demonstrations against oppressive laws.[46]

Roman women were expected to supervise the education of their children.[47] The education of women was valued in Roman society. It was possible for girls to attend school. Women studied music, philosophy, literature, grammar and geometry. Among the lower classes in Roman society women received a smaller allotment of grain than did men and boys. There were fewer restrictions on morality and marriage and less supervision.[48] Thus women in Roman society did exercise a public role. They held real political and economic power. Yet they were restricted for the most part from holding political offices. Women were always

---

[44] Ibid, pp. 5-29

[45] Ibid.

[46] Ibid.

[47] Elizabeth M. Tetlow, "The Status of Women in Greek, Roman and Jewish Society," www.womenpriests.org/classic/tetlow1.asp1980, pp. 5-29, [20.6.2017].

[48] Ibid, pp. 5-29.

legally and theoretically subordinate to men. Women of the upper classes were able to become well educated. This increased the possibility of their being respected by men. The status of women in Roman society was never in fact, however, equal to that of men.[49]

In Roman religion, women were excluded from the highest office.[50] Under the authority of the pontiffs were the vestal virgins, who had the task of tending the sacred hearth-fire of the state. The Romans considered this function so important that the welfare of the state was thought to depend upon it. One who was involved in sexual immorality, which was thought to pollute the cult, was buried alive. The vestal virgins were all daughters of patrician families until the time of Augustus. But most were by that time rather old to find a suitable marriage partner and preferred to continue in office where they enjoyed power and authority that increased with age and seniority. These vestal virgins were the only Roman women who were legally independent of the authority of the pater familias. Important political documents and wills were entrusted to their care. They sometimes even influenced emperors. The vestals were, however, always under the authority of the pontiff.[51]

The role of vestal virgins in the priesthood was a very important public role strictly for women in ancient Rome.[52] They were forbidden from marriage or sex for a period of thirty years, the vestals devoted themselves to the study and correct observance of rituals which were deemed necessary for the security and survival of Rome but which could not be performed by male colleagues or priests.[53]

---

[49] Ibid, pp. 5-29.

[50] Ibid, pp. 5-29.

[51] Ibid, pp. 5-29.

[52] Gregory S. Aldrete, www.the greatcoursedaily.com, [18.8.2020]

[53] en.m.wikipedia.org, [16.8.2020].

However, the cult of the Bona Dea admitted only women.[54] A woman magistrate presided over this cult and the vestal virgins also played a role in it. Some of the women's cults admitted only those of a certain social or marital class. The cults of Patrician Chastity and Womanly Fortune admitted only patrician women of no more than one husband (*univiri*). The cult of Plebian Chastity admitted *plebian univiri*. The cult of Virile Fortune was especially for prostitutes. These cults of Fortune and Chastity tended to reinforce traditional sex roles and mores for women.[55]

The Romans imported Greek priestesses for the Hellenistic mystery cult of Ceres and granted them Roman citizenship. This was a women's cult comprised of matrons and virgins. It excluded men and persons of the lower classes. They were women of both the upper and lower classes. This cult was considered revolutionary by the Roman authorities and it was suppressed several times.[56] Thus in the Roman empire women did exercise an official role in religion, although they were not admitted to the highest religious offices. Religion was ultimately controlled by men. Even cults admitting only women were frequently used by the male authorities to reinforce the subordinate role of women. Roman men and women were permitted to convert to new religions as long as these were not seen as threatening the well-being of the state.[57]

Women in Jewish Culture

Jewish women were looked upon as inferior. Judaism found some substantiation of that presumption by looking at the bodily marker of

---

[54] Ibid.

[55] Ibid, pp. 5-29.

[56] Elizabeth M. Tetlow, "The Status of Women in Greek, Roman and Jewish Society," pp. 5-29, www.womenpriests.org/classic/tetlow1.asp1980, [20.6.2017].

[57] Ibid.

circumcision. Men were set apart as Jewish by circumcision, but there was not a comparable bodily identification for Jewish women. For the rabbis, who considered the natural inferiority of women self-evident, the lack of a bodily sign was not problematic. Even later in Christianity, some considered that since femaleness was inescapable, the female salvation would always be somehow lesser than that of males.[58]

In Jewish culture, sexuality was also a very sensitive issue. This made women constitute an additional source of danger in rabbinic thinking and this led to social discrimination. It is from this background that rabbis formulated a law that women should be excluded from synagogue participation or should be seated separately during worship times. The Talmud states that the voice of a woman is indecent.[59] This idea emerges from the ruling that a man may not recite the *shema*[60] while he hears a woman singing, since her voice might divert his concentration from the prayer. Extrapolating from hearing to seeing, rabbinic prohibitions on male and female contact in worship eventually led to a physical barrier between men and women in the synagogue to preserve men from sexual distraction during prayer.[61] In addition, Tracey Rich says that it is of utmost importance that the separation of men and women during prayer be understood.[62] According to Jewish Law, men and women must be separated during prayer, usually by a wall or curtain called a *mechitzah* or by placing women on a second-floor balcony. There are two reasons for this: first, the man's mind is

---

[58] Svetlana Renee Papazov, "The Place of Women in the Graeco Roman World, " p. 2, http://enrichmentjournal. ag.org. [15.8.2016].

[59] *Babylonian Talmud*, Berakhoth 24a.

[60] It is the designed prayer, well written, usually to be recited or fluently read by an assigned man.

[61] Judith Baskin, "Women in Rabbinic Literature," p. 5, www.myjewishlearning.com/beliefs/Issues/Gender.

[62] Tracey R. Rich "The Role of Women," p. 2, www.jewfaq.org/copyright.htm, [19.4.2015].

supposed to be on prayer, not on the pretty girl praying near him. Second, many pagan-religious ceremonies at the time Judaism was founded involved sexual activity and orgies, and the separation prevented or at least discouraged this. Interestingly, although men should not be able to see women during prayer, women were permitted to see men during prayer. This seems to support the opinion that women are better able to concentrate on prayer while an attractive member of the opposite sex is visible. Inside the synagogue Jewish men only could enter and pray thanking God for creating them male. They thus prayed in this way:

> Blessed art thou, O Lord our God, King of the Universe, who has not made me a heathen. Blessed art thou, O Lord God our God, King of the universe, who has not made me a bondman. Blessed art thou, O Lord God our God, King of the universe, who hast not made me a woman.[63]

In this case when men prayed, women also prayed recognizing the will of the Lord on how He created them. These women believed that it is the Lord who opens the eyes of the blind. But in this case these blinds can both be men and women. I therefore find the prayer of women to be more humble, positive and liberating than the prayer of men. This is because men recognized it to be an advantage not to be created as a woman.[64] The men's prayer made women spiritually and physically inferior to them. But this was not God's intention in creation. He made them both in His own image, male and female (Gen 1:27; 5:1). Thus, a devout Jew saw a woman in a role that is strictly secondary to a man. She was inferior and subordinate to the man. In addition, the man's

---

[63] Beatrice S. Neall, "A Theology of Woman," in: Karen and Ron Flowers, *A Woman Place*, Hagerstown: Review and Herald, 1992, pp. 19, 81. This was a prayer also usually prayed outside the temple.

[64] Frank Chirwa, "A Critical Examination of the Changing Role of Women in the Seventh-day Adventist Church in Malawi: A Historical, Theological, and Social-Cultural Analysis," PhD, Mzuzu University, 2014, p. 275.

mind was believed to be active-superior-good and the woman's mind passive-inferior-bad.[65] Therefore, they were supposed to avoid the streets where they could fall under the gaze of men. Hence, women were supposed to time their visit to the temple so that they did it when most people had gone home.[66]

In the Second Temple, which was constructed after some Jews returned from exile in Babylon, there was a separate room for women. Even when Herod rebuilt it late in the first century BCE, one of its features was the women's court, which was considered the least sacred area. Next to it was the court of the male Israelites, followed by the court of Priests, and finally the Temple itself. The courts were laid out in this order to separate women as far as possible from men.[67]

Jewish culture sounds wholly arbitrary on women but critical analysis shows that women were accorded high respect in Jewish tradition as part of their ethnic culture.[68] Tracey Rich agrees with this fact and by comparison she states that Greek women were accorded a higher degree of respect than women of other pagan societies. He argues that even though Judaism did share the universal conception of the inferiority of women, it did not sanction the total subjection of women to men, but rather sought to elevate women in their proper sphere. She further observes that neither was there in Judaism the separation of sexes so common among other peoples, for Hebrew women mixed

---

[65] Philo, "Philo," F. H. Colson and G. H. Whitaker (trs), *The Loeb Classical Library*, Harvard: University Press, 1949.

[66] Ibid.

[67] "The Status of Women in the Hebrew Scriptures," p. 5, www.religioustolerance.org/hom_bibg.htm, [19.4.2015].

[68] Tracey R. Rich, "The Role of Women, " p. 1, www.jewfaq.org/copyright.htm, [19.4.2015].

more freely and often took a positive and influential part in both public and private affairs.[69]

In intellectual pursuits and the study of the Torah, women earned merit by sending their male children to learn in the synagogue, and their husbands to study in the schools of the rabbis, and by waiting for their husbands until they return from the schools of the rabbis.[70] Judith Narrowe states that in the pre-Enlightenment times, Jewish women received no formal religious education and were most often unaware of the content and meaning of Jewish classic texts.[71] They were thus not familiar with the discussions and explanations of the rabbis regarding the *Mitzvoth*. Craig Keener concurs with her that women were less likely to be literate than men; were trained in philosophy far less often than men; were trained in rhetoric almost never; and in Judaism they were far less likely to be educated in the law.[72] Women were discouraged from pursuing higher education or religious pursuits, but this seems to be primarily because women who engaged in such pursuits might neglect their primary duties as wives and mothers at home.[73] Because this thought was well established in their minds, rabbis believed that anyone who taught his wife or daughter the Torah taught her lasciviousness. It is stated in the Mishnah that the Torah and the wife were believed to be structural allomorphs and separated realms to be highly valued but also to be kept separate.[74] The Mishnah is the book

---

[69] Oswald Jimmy Banda, "The Role of Women in the Anglican Diocese of Northern Malawi," MA, Mzuzu University, 2013, p. 27.

[70] *Babylonian Talmud*, Berakhoth 17a.

[71] Narrowe, Judith "The Role of Women in Jewish Religious Education," July 2000, http://www.wcc.coe. org/wcc/English.

[72] Craig S. Keener, *The IVP Bible Background Commentary, New Testament, An Indispensable Resource for all Students of the Bible,* Downers Grove, Illinois: InterVarsity, 1993, p. 611.

[73] Tracey R. Rich, "The Role of Women," p. 1, www.jewfaq.org/copyright.htm.

[74] Mishnah Sotah 3:4.

containing the body of Jewish rabbinical tradition.[75] Nkhoma asserts that "The Mishnah is a deposit of Jewish religious and cultural practice that cuts across four centuries and has substantial amount of pre-Christian traditional material."[76] Some information from this book shows that in a Jewish tradition a man controlled the earnings of his wife.[77] It is said of a woman that her idleness was tantamount to unchastity. Thus, everything found by a woman in her labouring belonged to the husband. Also, during her lifetime, the man who looked after her had the right to the use of her inheritance.[78] Relating to marriage, after two years staying with a barren wife, the man was allowed to divorce her.[79] Men were also not expected to be seen talking to a woman. This would disturb them from meditating and studying the law, hence, lead to their destruction.[80]

Women's obligations and responsibilities were different from men's responsibilities. In the job assignment, women were assigned to the home, a very important place. We may look at the home responsibility as inferior but Jews esteemed it highly. Tracey Rich writes that in traditional Judaism, the primary role of a woman is wife and mother, keeper of the household.[81] However, Judaism has great respect for the importance of that role and the spiritual influence that the woman has

---

[75] Evelyn and Frank Stagg, *Women in the World of Jesus,* Edinburgh: Westminster, 1978, p. 49.

[76] Jonathan Nkhoma, *The Use of Fulfilment Quotations in the Gospel according to Matthew*, Zomba: Kachere, 2005, p. 45.

[77] Evelyn and Frank Stagg, *Women in the World of Jesus,* Edinburgh: Westminster, 1978, p. 49.

[78] Ibid, p. 51.

[79] Ibid, p. 50

[80] Ibid, p. 52.

[81] Tracey R. Rich, "The Role of Women," p. 1, www.jewfaq.org/copyright.htm, [16.8.2016].

over her family. The Talmud says that when a pious man marries a wicked woman, the man becomes wicked, but when a wicked man marries a pious woman, the man becomes pious.[82] The bible also testifies to this fact when it describes what happened to King Solomon when he married seven hundred wives and three hundred concubines including the daughter of Pharaoh. These women were drawn from the Moabites, Ammonites, Edomites, Sidonians, and Hittites who later turned Solomon's heart after other gods.[83] Judaism put much emphasis on raising children well in the home under a spiritual woman. Therefore, women were busy people in the home and could not be very active in the temple or synagogue. After all, a woman could not be expected to just drop a crying baby when the time came to perform a religious assignment. Concerning women's education and the study of the Torah, Papazov argues that girls learned to read and write only if someone at home taught them. Women were especially likely to know the rules for keeping their household, particularly in Pharisaic families. In times of worship, synagogue worship was pro-men and did not allow women to speak because Jewish women were barred from public speaking.[84] Jewish women were, therefore, not allowed to reason with their husbands. Their part was obedience in all things husbands or men required of them.

Women were exempted from performing some religious commandments because of the nature of their work.[85] It is this exemption from certain commandments that has led to the greatest misunderstanding of the role of women in Jewish religion. Scholars who have written

---

[82] *Babylonian Talmud*, Shabbat 62a.

[83] 1 Kings 11:1-13.

[84] Svetlana Renee Papazov, "The Place of Women in the Graeco Roman World, " Texas, p. 2, http://enrichment journal.ag.org, [16.8.2016].

[85] For example, women were not obligated to attend morning and evening prayers. Even if they attended, they were not obligated to recite the *mitzvoth*.

negatively about women's exemption think that the exemption is a prohibition. On the contrary, although women were not obligated to perform time-based commandments at specific times, they were generally permitted to observe such commandments if they chose to. Furthermore, because this exemption diminished the role of women in the synagogue, some bible scholars perceive that women had no role in Jewish religious life. This misconception derives from the assumption that Jewish religious life revolved around the synagogue. It did not. It revolved around the home where the woman's role was in every bit as important as the man's. This situation is still prevalent today.[86]

The social status of Jewish women in Palestine during the Graeco-Roman period had an image of its own. This status was not only shaped by the prevalent culture of the ruling empire, but also strongly influenced by religious norms and expectations. Papazov cites Judaism, and later Christianity, which had put their formative stamps on the identities of the Jewish women.[87] These distinctions show that women were treated differently on account of circumstances not of their making. Jewish women had rights as well. They had the right to buy, sell, and own property, and make their own contracts. They had the right to do business to give supplies to their families. They had the right to be consulted with regard to marriage issues. They were not forced into marriage. Also, marital sex was regarded as the woman's right, and not the man's. They were protected by the Law so that men were forbidden to beat and mistreat their wives. This shows that Judaism was not always negative on women.[88] Such rights are often neglected by biblical scholars who comment on the subject of women in Judaism. Jews were

---

[86] Tracey R. Rich, "The Role of Women," p. 2, www.jewfaq.org/copyright.htm, accessed on [15.8.2016].

[87] Svetlana Renee Papazov, "The Place of Women in the Graeco Roman World," Texas, p. 2, http://enrichmentjournal.ag, [16.8.2016].

[88] Ibid, p. 8.

the custodian of the Torah,[89] and their religion was anchored on the Torah. As a matter of system, the responsibility of teaching, interpreting, defending, and safeguarding the Law or Torah was given to very prominent and influential figures called rabbis. They were lawyers as well as determinants of gender activities. Judith Baskin[90] sheds more light on their role when she states that rabbis of the Talmud[91] designated specific female roles and activities, and were wary

---

[89] The first five books of the Old Testament sometimes called the Law or the Pentateuch.

[90] Judith Baskin is the Director of the Harold Schnitzer Family Program in Judaic Studies and a Professor of Religious Studies at the University of Oregon.

[91] The Talmud (Hebrewתַּלְמוּד meaning "instruction, learning, teaching, study") is a central text of mainstream Judaism. It takes the form of a record of rabbinic discussions pertaining to Jewish law, ethics, philosophy, customs, and history. The Talmud is the scholarly commentary by rabbis on the Mishnah. There are two types of Talmuds; the Palestinian and Babylonian Talmuds. The Palestinian Talmud was one of the two compilations of Jewish religious teachings and commentary that was transmitted orally for centuries prior to its compilation by Jewish scholars in Israel. It is a compilation of teachings of the schools of Tiberias, Sepphoris and Caesarea. It is written largely in a western Aramaic dialect that differs from its Babylonian counterpart. The Babylonian Talmud was compiled about the year 500 CE, although it continued to be edited later. The word "Talmud," when used without qualification, usually refers to the Babylonian Talmud.

The Mishnah, the first great written code of Oral Law, contains the sayings of authoritative rabbis. It is a book of legal directives compiled in the second century CE by Jewish sages in the land of Israel. It is a compilation of legal opinions and debates. Statements in the Mishnah are typically terse, recording brief opinions of the rabbis debating a subject; or recording only an unattributed ruling, apparently representing a consensus view. The rabbis recorded in the Mishnah are known as Tannaim. Since it sequences its laws by subject matter instead of by biblical context, the Mishnah discusses individual subjects thoroughly and it includes a much broader selection of halakhic subjects than the Midrash. The Mishnah's topical organization thus became the framework of the Talmuds. But not every tractate in the Mishnah has a corresponding Talmud. Also, the order of the tractates in the Talmud differs in some cases from that in the Mishnah.

of women's nature.[92] Consistent with the times in which they lived, rabbis prescribed limited roles for women in religious and communal life. Judith Baskin assumes that this certainty of a woman's ancillary place in the scheme of things permeated rabbinic thinking. She says that the male sages apportioned separate spheres and responsibilities to women and men, making every effort to confine women to the private realms of the family. She suggests that Jews placed women in the secondary and ancillary position because of the part Eve played in the dramatic fall of humanity in the Garden of Eden.[93] Ellen G. White dismisses this when she says that Adam had equally the freedom of choice as Eve. He could have chosen not to partake of the forbidden fruit that Eve brought to him. She says that it is, therefore, proper to suggest that he deliberately chose to sin against God. She concludes that it would be somewhat unfair to put the blame on Eve alone when each one of them was given, by the same God, an equal opportunity to exercise freedom of choice.[94] It would, therefore, be justifiable, according to Ellen G. White, to assume that while God abhors sin, he may not go to the extent of cursing a woman and reduce her to that low status as the Jews had done, upholding the man who not only sinned but sinned by choice.

Even though Jewish women were confined to private realms of the family during the Roman era, there were also a number of minor roles they played in public life. Their obligations included economic activities that would benefit the household, so that undertaking business transactions with other individuals in private and public markets was an expected part of a woman's domestic role. Their central role in the

---

[92] Judith R. Baskin, "Women in Rabbinic Literature," p. 1, www.myjewish-learning.com/beliefs/Issues/Gender, [16.8.2016].

[93] Ibid, p. 4.

[94] Ellen G. White, *The History of Redemption*, Seoul: Everlasting Gospel Publishing Association, 2008, p. 24.

community was basically to look after their families. They were allowed to meet in gatherings with other women, and attend social events. Judith Baskin says that whatever women did in public, they did as private individuals.[95] Not only by custom but as a result of detailed legislation, women were excluded from significant participation in most of rabbinic society's communal and power-conferring public activities. Since these endeavours had mostly to do with participation in religious services, communal study of biblical texts, and the execution of judgments under Jewish law, women were simultaneously isolated from access to public authority and power and from the communal, spiritual and intellectual sustenance available to men. Violation of this custom would be looked upon as disgraceful and would bring reproach upon the Jewish religion.[96] Jewish women were obligated to strictly keep this custom wherever they could be as their identity. As long as women satisfied male expectations in their family assigned roles, they were revered and honoured for enhancing the lives of their families and particularly for enabling their male relatives to fulfill their religious obligations.[97]

Women in the Qumran Community

It was this kind of defilement of women that extended to the Qumran community, linking it to the New Testament period. The Qumran community saw themselves as medium of revelation and teacher of the Law. At this time, their rivals were the Pharisees. The Pharisees were a lay-oriented movement concerned to apply the Law to the whole of Israel. They aimed at bringing Israel under the cultic regulations for

---

[95] Judith R. Baskin, "Women in Rabbinic Literature," p. 2, www.myjewish-learning.com/beliefs/Issues/Gender, [16.8.2016].

[96] *Seventh-day Adventist Bible Commentary*, Hagerstown: Review & Herald, vol. 6, Acts to Ephesians, 1980, p. 793.

[97] Judith R. Baskin, "Women in Rabbinic Literature," p. 3, www.myjewishlearning.com/beliefs/Issues/Gender_and_Feminism, [16.8.2016].

holiness.[98] While the Qumran Essenes never thought of including women in priestly ministry because of the same laws of uncleanness, the Pharisees made it even more difficult for women, confirming the pattern that was already set.[99] The further challenge was that women in Israel were kept at a distance from the centre of holiness. They were denied access to the court of the Jewish men as well as the Holy Place. The main reasons were again menstruation and child bearing.[100] Also, the Qumran community, the Essenes, never took a wife because women were thought to be selfish, excessively jealous and skilful in ensnaring the morals of a spouse as well as seducing him by endless charms.[101] So, the Essene literature of Qumran is quite negative both toward women and sex. It was a celibate community which was dominated by priests. There was no real place for women either theologically or in the reality of its existence in the desert wilderness of Judaea.[102]

Josephus' Views on Women

Josephus also reflects a male bias in his writings. He confirmed that the Essenes wished to protect themselves against women's wantonness. They were persuaded that none of the women kept their plighted troth

---

[98] Jacob Neusner, *Understanding Rabbinic Judaism from Talmudic to Modern Times*, New York: KTAV Publishing House, 1974, pp. 12-15; See also his book, *From Politics to Piety: The Emergence of Pharisaic Judaism*, Upper Saddle River: Prentice-Hall, 1973, p. 83.

[99] Evelyn and Frank Stagg, *Women in the World of Jesus*, Edinburgh: Westminster, 1978, p. 31.

[100] Jacob Neusner, *Understanding Rabbinic Judaism from Talmudic to Modern Times*, New York: KTAV Publishing House, 1974, pp. 12-15, and his *From Politics to Piety: The Emergence of Pharisaic Judaism*, Upper Saddle River: Prentice-Hall, 1973.

[101] A. Dupont-Sommer, *The Essene Writings from Qumran*, tr. by G. Vermes, Oxford: Basil Blackwell, 1961, pp. 295-305.

[102] Elizabeth Tetlow, "The Status of Women in Greek, Roman and Jewish Society," pp. 5-29, www.womenpriests.org/classic/tetlow1.asp1980, [20.6. 2017].

to one man.[103] Thus, Josephus generally refers to the womanly character in negative terms by comparing it to what Potiphar's wife did, when she tried to seduce Joseph. He affirms that such a wicked and adulterous wife portrays the general behaviour of all women.[104] Furthermore, Josephus records that women were excluded as witnesses in Jewish courts. This law said, "From women let no evidence be accepted, because of the levity and temerity of their sex."[105] He also reveals that in the Temple ministry women were segregated, due to defilement by menstruation. They were also supposed to sit in their own court, even if they were not menstruating. Even the gates were segregated. Women were supposed to enter the women's court only through the south and north gates.[106] Josephus equally accepted the theoretical inferiority of women. While living within the Roman Empire, he described a number of influential women in his historical works. He made note of the quite normal resentment of Alexandra, the mother of Mariamne, at Herod's restriction of her freedom. On the other hand, he reiterated that women could not be witnesses and were segregated during worship. It is the Jewish view of woman that emerges as dominant in the thought of Josephus:

> The woman, says the Law, is in all things inferior to the man. Let her accordingly be submissive, not for her humiliation, but that she may be directed; for the authority has been given by God to the man.[107]

---

[103] Flavius Josephus, "Josephus,"(trs) H. St. J. Thackery et al, *Loeb Classical Library*, vol. 2, Harvard: University, 1965, p. 8.

[104] Ibid, p. 6.

[105] Ibid, p. 8.

[106] Ibid, vol. 5, p. 5.

[107] Elizabeth M. Tetlow, "The Status of Women in Greek, Roman and Jewish Society," pp. 5-29, www.womenpriests.org/classic /tetlow1.asp1980, [20.6. 2017].

Conclusion

This chapter has established that the position of women in the Greco-Roman World differed from culture to culture. Women in classical Greece did have some education and some role in society. Both were likely to be greater if they did not live in Athens. However, neither their education nor their social role was equal to that of men of the same socio-economic class. Women did not have the freedom to determine their own lives. There was a saying in ancient Greece, at various times attributed to Thales, Socrates and Plato, in which man thanked the gods, that he was not uncivilized, a slave, or a woman. However, women in Roman society did exercise a public role and held political and economic power. Also, the Roman women did exercise an official role in religion, although they were not admitted to the highest religious offices. Religion was ultimately controlled by men. Even cults admitting only women were frequently used by the male authorities to reinforce the subordination of women. Roman men and women were permitted to convert to new religions as long as these were not seen as threatening the the state. Yet women were restricted for the most part from holding political offices. Women were always legally and theoretically subordinate to men. Women of the upper classes were able to become well educated. This increased the possibility of their being respected by men. However, the status of women in Roman society was never in fact equal to that of men, and women were nowhere totally free or equal. Yet Hellenistic and Roman women did enjoy some degree of freedom and exercised a real political, economic, and religious role in their societies. First century Judaism lived in the cultural milieu of Hellenism. It was unable to ignore secular culture, but had to react to it. Christianity was born into this complex syncretistic world. The societies of this world still by and large advocated the traditional role of subordination and silence of women as the ideal. Yet in real life the women of history were neither subordinate nor silent. The ideal was challenged in the forum of real life. The tension and conflict generated by this challenge were the social milieu in which New Testament Christianity was formulated.

Chapter 4

Gender Theology in Pauline Literature

Introduction

Since the previous chapter has given us the broader context in which Paul worked and ascertained the cultural disparities in the Greco-Roman World, it is now pertinent to understand the Pauline Texts in their literary context. This chapter is to provide an analysis of these texts to establish his gender theology in light of his letters to the Galatians, the Corinthians and Timothy. Also, this chapter offers a discussion of these difficult passages. In order to understand these passages, I will start the discussions with Galatians 3:28 and 1 Corinthians 11:2-16 before considering 1 Corinthians 14:34-35 and 1 Timothy 2:11-12. Some scholars have argued that Galatians was Paul's first letter and 1 Corinthians 11 forms a good background to understanding other difficult Pauline texts.

Much commendable work has been done by many biblical scholars and theologians in an attempt to unveil the theology of Apostle Paul on women, as taught in these texts, including Galatians 3:28. Interpretations vary considerably on this matter and much debate is still going on. Perspectives probably differ mainly because of the differing biblical hermeneutical approaches scholars use. Our starting point is to provide an analysis of these texts in their contexts using the Historical-Critical approach.

Women in Galatians 3:28

Brief Analysis of the Letter to the Galatians

The Epistle to the Galatians, most likely the first of Paul's letters, calls the attention of the reader toward two dominant themes: the justification of the believer in the Lord Jesus Christ apart from legal works and the ministry of the Holy Spirit as the indwelling energizer of the spiritual life in Christ. Commentators on the letter have generally agreed that it falls into three sections. The opening two chapters are largely personal, containing a defense of his gospel and apostleship. The following section, also of two chapters, contains the exposition, in strongly argumentative form, of the heart of his gospel, the doctrine of justification by faith alone apart from legal works. The letter's final two chapters conclude with a hortatory appeal to practice the principles and responsibilities of the Christian life through the energy of the indwelling Spirit of God.[1]

Brief Historical Context of Galatians

The Galatians were Gauls living in the Roman province of Galatia. They can be described as once barbarians, without an encouraging history, one branch of which Julius Caesar knew in France as the Gauls.[2] These Gauls were distinguished from the West-European Gauls by the term *"Gallo-Graecians"* from which the name Galatians comes. With the coming of the Romans, conditions did not change markedly for the Galatians.[3] It is to these Gentiles that Paul came for missions on his first missionary journey and where he planted churches. When Paul left, some Jews who claimed to be Christians from Jerusalem came to Galatia but with a different gospel. They had a Judaic kind of worship even after converting to Christianity. In many instances, they had carried on with their Jewish tradition wherever they moved. In general, the Jews regarded themselves as religiously very important. In this instance, they felt themselves superior seeing that they were coming from the great city of Jerusalem that bore such a religious significance. Jerusalem was

---

[1] Lewis Johnson, "Role Distinctions in the Church Galatians 3: 28," in John Piper and Wayne Grudem, *Recovering Biblical Manhood & Womanhood,* Wheaton: Crossway, 1991, pp. 154-164.

[2] Frank E. Gaebelein (ed), *The Expositor's Bible Commentary with NIV,* Vol. 10, Grand Rapids: Zondervan, 1976, p. 407.

[3] Ibid, p. 407.

the place of God.⁴ The primary focus of much of the letter is a problem Paul refers to once, perhaps a little loosely, as 'Judaizing' (2:14). He means by this the wholesale adoption of traditional Jewish practices by his Gentile converts in Galatia. In effect, they are to become Jews, although they will probably retain many of their Christian commitments. Suffice it to say that Paul seems unambiguously opposed to this step, and deploys various arguments designed to dissuade his audience from taking it.⁵

Exegesis of Galatians 3:28

The important point is that we must first understand Paul's counsels in their original setting. Any attempt to understand this verse requires that we first know the practice of the Galatian worshippers. In this passage Paul tackles the problem of ethnic, social and sexual divisions in the Galatian society. Paul is saying here that all who were divided in the society of his day can be united in Christ. What was to determine identity and status was Christ and whether one was in his body.⁶ So what does it mean to be in Christ and how is that different from being a part of any other group in the Greco-Roman World?⁷ Women could assume roles other than wife or mother in the Christian community. We need to take note of not only Paul's position but also the direction of his remarks as a strong feminist.⁸ The considerable evidence about women in the Pauline churches indicates that Paul was indeed open to women's

---

[4] Bert Jan Peerbolte, "Paul and the Law: Introduction Course on Paul, NT 2 Class notes," *JMTC*, 2008.

[5] Douglas A. Campbell, "The Logic of Eschatology; The Implication of Paul's Gospel for Gender as Suggested by Galatians 3:28a in Context," in Douglas A. Campbell (ed), *Gospel and Gender: A Trinitarian Engagement with being Male and Female in Christ*, New York: T&T Clark, 2003, pp. 58-81, esp. p. 59.

[6] Ben Witheringstone, *The Paul Quest: The Renewed Search for the Jew of Tarsus*, Downers Grove: InterVarsity, 1998, p. 220.

[7] Ibid, p. 219.

[8] Ibid, p. 224.

playing a variety of roles in the Church. Although, the discussion usually comes down to texts like 1 Corinthians 11:2-16,14:33-35 and even 1 Timothy 2:11-12, whatever the limitations Paul is imposing in these texts cannot be interpreted to refer to a global silencing of women in the church.[9]

Interpretations of Galatians 3:28

Some scholars assert that clearer statements concerning the role of women which are found in Paul's other writings must be given more weight than the passing comment of Galatians 3:28, and they expound this verse in its context in the Epistle to the Galatians to show that it cannot carry the doctrinal and relational burden which is being placed upon it.[10] Our approach to understanding this verse is to investigate its context and to give grounds for rejecting more extreme positions adopted by some scholars. I argue that Galatians 3:28 in context is radical, abolitionist, and therefore political and a liberating text.[11]

There is a misunderstanding of the religious activities of women in the Greco-Roman world today. To understand Paul, one has to know the Greco-Roman cults of women.[12] It is at this point that we are least capable of understanding the reasoning of the Apostle to the Gentiles. He notes that the realms of male and female religion frequently represented diverse and disparate worlds, often separated by suspicion

---

[9] Ibid, p. 225. This is the position I share in understanding Paul's gender theology as noted by Ben Witheringstone.

[10] Ward Powers, *The Ministry of Women in the Church*, Adelaide: SPCKA, 1996, p. 113.

[11] Douglas A. Campbell, "The Logic of Eschatology; The Implication of Paul's Gospel for Gender as Suggested by Galatians 3:28a in Context," in Douglas A. Campbell (ed), *Gospel and Gender: A Trinitarian Engagement with being Male and Female in Christ*, New York: T&T Clark, 2003, pp. 58-81, esp. p. 69.

[12] Catherine Kroeger, "The Apostle Paul and the Greco-Roman World Cults of Women," 30-1-pp. 25-38 (Paul and the Cults of Women), March 1987, pp. 25-38, esp. p. 28.

and hostility. Frequently women worshiped different deities from men, in different temples and on different days. Feminine religiosity was quite different from its masculine counterpart.[13] Yet, Paul viewed the Church as a body containing Jew and Gentile, slave and free, male and female (Gal 3:28). This required serious readjustment whether one was formerly an observant Jew, a philosophical Greek, or a member of a disadvantaged class of society. Conversion to a new deity did not necessarily alter one's former attitudes and practices. The assimilation of former pagan women would pose special difficulties. It is noteworthy that the Pauline dictates regarding women are directed to troubled Gentile Churches with serious problems involving religiously undesirable elements. These dictates should be studied in the context of the phenomena associated with the cults and practices of ancient women.[14]

In Gal 3:28 Paul not only claims that there are no longer male and female, but also that men and women are one in Christ, raising the question of what this would have meant for women converts to become members of the community of Jesus followers but also to have their female bodies become one in the male Christ?[15] Sexuality, to use a modern word, was understood in the Greco-Roman world as a continuum of possibilities rather than as a stark contrast between male and female. Unlike the modern notion of a horizontal continuum for gender and sexuality, a hierarchy with a clear top and bottom positioned the male end of the spectrum as exercising a natural dominance over the female end. Masculinity was associated with strength, rationality, self-control, activity, and perfection, and contrasted with weakness, sexuality and procreation, passion, passivity,

---

[13] Ibid, p. 28.

[14] Ibid, p. 28.

[15] Jeremy Punt, "Post-Apartheid Racism in South Africa: The Bible, Social Identity and Stereotyping," *RT* 16, nos. 3-4, 2009, pp. 246-272.

and imperfection which were associated with the feminine. Jeremy Punt observes that a body necessarily consisted of male and female aspects, and the location of a particular person at a specific point on the male-female axis depended on the relative strength of these aspects.[16]

Galatians 3:28 is clearly Paul's most radical statement about gender identity and roles: "There is neither Jew nor Greek, neither slave nor free, neither male nor female, for you all are one in Christ Jesus." Judith Gandry-Volf develops an exegetical argument in dialogue with two recent major discussions of gender identity in early Christianity that reflect the 'abolition of differences' interpretation of Galatians 3:28: Antoinette Clark Wire's *The Corinthian Women Prophets: A Reconstruction through Paul's Rhetoric (1990),* and Daniel Boyarin's *A Radical Jew: Paul and the Politics of Identity (1994)* have pointed to the significance of Gal 3:28 for women at Corinth. She argues that these two are representative of the dominant trend in reading Paul with a cluster of interrelated questions surrounding the topic of 'Christ and gender, the questions of difference, sameness, equality, hierarchy and unity as these relate to the character of Christ and salvation.' She examines the two and summarizes their positions as: They both not only presuppose that in Paul's mind the erasure of difference is needed to achieve equality and, inversely, the affirmation of differences is construed to entail hierarchy, Paul understands the ideal state which is to be realized eschatologically as a state of such equality with all differences erased, agree on mechanism by which equality is achieved but also construe the problem Paul is dealing with and therefore the solution he is offering along the categorical axis of 'sameness and differences.' Difference is the problem Paul is combating because it entails hierarchy; sameness is

---

[16] Ibid.
[16] Ibid.

the solution Paul is offering because it entails equality. She challenges all these four positions and provides her own position.[17]

The context in which the statement 'there is no male and female' is embedded does not make immediately clear what those words mean. Even if we accept that Galatians is indeed concerned with sexuality and gender issues, we will still have to conclude that Paul nowhere in this letter explains what he means by 'there is no male and female.' Even the baptismal formula is found in the concluding part of Paul's argument in 3:6-29. She contends that Paul uses the circumcision saying to indicate the meaning of the traditional saying in Gal 3:28. In the formula, Paul is also referring to the adiaphorization of traditional religio-ethnic identity markers.[18] Possibly Paul intended in this way to rule out interpretations of the baptismal formula that he regarded as illegitimate. But the immediate context of Gal 3:28 suggests that the assertion 'there is neither Jew nor Greek', is not about erasure of differences but about revalorization of differences. For the new unity and equality of the community is attained not through the elimination of differences but through their revalorization.[19] Instead the possibility presents itself that the reference to 'no male and female' refers to the adiaphorization of sexual difference in the new creation in Christ. Distinct sexual identities would remain significant in some sense, but

---

[17] Judith M. Gundry-Volf, "Beyond Difference? Paul's Vision of a New Humanity in Galatians 3:28," in Douglas A. Campbell (ed), *Gospel and Gender: A Trinitarian Engagement with being Male and Female in Christ*, New York: T&T Clark, 2003, pp. 8-36, esp. 8-16.

[18] To adiaphorize means to make an existing reality to be irrelevant to the faith. For a detailed discussion see: Klaus Fiedler, *Christianity and African Culture: Conservative German Protestant Missionaries in Tanzania*. Blantyre: CLAIM-Kachere, 1999, pp. 36-37.

[19] Judith M. Gundry-Volf, "Beyond Difference? Paul's Vision of a New Humanity in Galatians 3:28," pp. 18-21.

lose their significance with respect to salvation and participation in the eschatological people of God.[20]

She investigates the Christological basis of equality in Gal 3:28 using soteriological terms to establish whether Paul conceives of salvation in analogy to the Hellenistic abolition of all differences and of merging into undifferentiated oneness. The 'You are Christ's (*ei de umeis christou*) in 3:29 underlies the abiding difference of the believer and Christ. It also suggests what kind of relation to Christ is the essence of Paul's argument. The ' baptism into Christ' statement conveyed by the words *eis Christon ebaptisthete* in 3:27, if understood in local sense ('baptized into Christ'), might be taken to connote passage into a kind of union with Christ through baptism that implies the erasure of differences. The non-local sense of *eis* in the unabbreviated version of the formula is determinative for use in the abbreviated version. We should take the expression *eis Christon ebaptisthete* in Gal 3:28 not as having a local sense but as having the connotation of belonging to Christ. A transmutation into Christ through baptism that erases creaturely differences is not implied. The 'In Christ Jesus' phrase i.e. *en Christo Jesou* is used twice in 3:26-28: once after the opening with the Christological claim in 3:26, 'You all are sons of God through faith', and the second time after the climactic statement in 3:28, "You all are one". Thus, neither 'in Christ' nor the similar 'in the Lord' formula implies erasure of differences in the flesh. This shows that the two phrases are not different in meaning.[21] Although the analysis of these Christological phases might appear to be correct, Gundry-Volf does not demonstrate why Paul used these Christological phrases. The point that Paul is using in his rhetorical argument to the Galatian Christians is a responsive, inclusive and liberating premise that they are all one in Christ. Hence,

---

[20] Ibid, p. 22.

[21] Ibid, p. 28.

ethnicity, gender and power should not divide them but that they should live Christ-like.

Gundry-Volf rightly argues that the line of Paul's reasoning from the problem to the solution, it does not run from 'difference' to 'undifferentiated unity,' but from 'sameness in sin despite outward differences' to 'unity with outward differences' in Christ. Therefore, her basic argument has been that Paul's claim in Gal 3:28, 'there is no male and female', in no way implies that the differences between male and female have been abolished. Instead, these differences have been adiaphorized: First, the problem is located not in the differences themselves, but behind them, in the commonality of sin and second, the solution is found outside of the differences, in the common faith in Christ that creates unity and equality of all. In Paul, we are witnessing a model of thought in which unity does not presuppose all-out sameness, dissolution of femininity or/and masculinity, but sameness in some respects, with respect to sin and with respect to the way of salvation.[22] I therefore argue that CCAP Zambia should emulate Paul's model of achieving an all-inclusive "sameness" Church by working out their differences to enhance gender equality. Thus, those who are reading Gal 3:28 and other Pauline texts that seem oppressive, are not reading Galatians correctly. This text is liberating and all other Pauline texts should be read in the light of Gal 3:28.

Galatians 3:26-29 is Paul's attempt to provide the means of bringing unity as verse 26 says. In verse 27, Paul shows how unity can be expressed, followed by the benefits of unity in verses 28 and 29. All believers become one in Christ. There are no racial boundaries, nor social boundaries, nor gender boundaries for the believer in Christ. Having become one with God, believers belong to each other in such a way that the distinctions that formerly divided them lose their significance. God does not see human distinctions. The believers attain

---

[22] Ibid, pp. 34-36.

a unity that was impossible under the previous covenant relationships. Both male and female of all races are children of God. Regarding salvation, there is no difference between male and female; we are all equal. Men and women who put trust in Christ stand to one another as brothers and sisters in the Lord. Hence a common faith imparts the basis for communion and harmony.[23] Therefore, salvation is not only doing something but knowing Jesus Christ. Husbands should respect their wives as joint heirs of salvation. The text encourages humility towards other Christians, no matter whom they are. It is not about our status, culture, creed or race. It is all about the faith in Christ Jesus that brings salvation. Johnson argues that, "There can be no doubt that Paul's statements have social and political implications of even a revolutionary dimension."[24]

I argue that verse 28 points to the human distinctions of race, social rank, and sex, distinctions that are in some sense nullified in Christ. Concerning this last antithesis, Bruce comments, "It is not their distinctiveness, but their inequality of religious role, that is abolished 'in Christ Jesus.'" He insists that the denial of discrimination holds good for the new existence 'in Christ' in its entirety although he admits that circumcision involved a form of discrimination against women that was removed in its demotion from the position of religious law. But he admits that other inequalities among Jewish and particularly among Gentile women existed. He then argues that, if leadership can be given to Gentiles and to slaves in the church fellowship, why not to women? Certainly, Paul welcomed the service of women in the Gentile mission (cf. Philippians 4:3) and permitted their exercise of prayer and prophecy in church gatherings. Bruce does appear to admit that other Pauline

---

[23] Lewis Johnson, "Role Distinctions in the Church: Galatians 3:28," in John Piper and Wayne Grudem, *Recovering Biblical Manhood and Womanhood*, Wheaton: Crossway Books, 1991, pp. 154-164.

[24] Ibid.

passages may provide restrictions on the role of women, but he contends that such passages "are to be understood in relation to Gal 3:28, and not vice versa."[25]

When one reads Paul's cry for equality in Gal 3:28, one cannot help but notice that Paul hopes for liberation from each of the three categories, race, gender, and master/slave relationships. However, he is immediately restricted by his own ideology of slavery and women and he is unable to bring the liberation to completion. Paul situates himself as a slave (1:10) earlier on in the letter as he is battling against those who would enslave Christians into observance of the Jewish Torah (Gal 3:19-23). Paul associates submission to the law with being slaves to the elements of the world (4:3, 9). Liberation was not defined by autonomous rights and privileges, but rather by servanthood to a master who was worthy of loyalty and honour. Paul found such a master in Jesus Christ.[26]

The key to Gal 3:28 is its interpretation in terms of the inclusion of women. From the evidence of Paul's letters, it is clear that he accepted slavery, though he never commended it.[27] He asserts that "though a social reality, this reality cannot be seen as good and commendable" and must therefore be challenged from the systematic statement of Paul. The same is true of women's liberation. The church today should not strive to maintain the status quo of church life in the first century, as though it were normative for all time. Rather, the church should seek to implement fully the principle that in Christ women are truly free.

---

[25] F.F. Bruce, *The Epistle to the Galatians: A Commentary on the Greek Text*. Grand Rapids: Eerdmans, 1982, pp. 185-187.

[26] Musa Dube, *Postcolonial Feminist Interpretation of the Bible,* St. Louis: Chalice, 2008, pp. 336-362.

[27] Klaus Fiedler, "Gender Equality in the New Testament: The Case of St Paul," in Klaus Fiedler, *Conflicted Power in Malawian Christianity,* Mzuzu: Mzuni Press, 2016, pp. 160-177.

Such an effort will contribute to the liberation of all mankind, both men and women.[28] Klaus Fiedler argues that the same reasoning should be applied to the statement that there is neither male nor female. There may be room for accepting social restrictions and for giving advice within that framework, like Paul may have done in 1 Corinthians and 1 Timothy. But general conclusions cannot be based on an ancient pastoral adaptation to a given culture, but must be based on the authoritative statements in scripture. In that process, a study of the women's role in the early church in a historic way can help clarify what belongs to the systematic side of Paul's teaching and what belongs to the pastoral side. Just as much as slaves in their days were right in reading Gal 3:28 as a powerful critique of existing conditions in church and society,[29] the CCAP Zambia can also find in them a unique window to understand Pauline texts, particularly those that seem to be restricting participation of women in the church.

The fact that both men and women are said by scripture to be created in the "image of God" should exclude all feelings of pride or inferiority and any idea that one sex is "better" or "worse" than the other. Galatians 3:27-28 emphasizes that equality in status among God's people must not be forgotten. Men should not think that they have greater importance than women or that they are of superior value before God; nor should women think themselves inferior or less important in the church. Rather both men and women are equal in importance and value to God and equal in membership in Christ's body, the church, for all eternity.[30] In practical terms, this means that no one

---

[28] Ward Powers, *The Ministry of Women in the Church*, Adelaide: SPCKA, 1996, p. 117.

[29] Klaus Fiedler, "Gender Equality in the New Testament: The Case of St Paul," in Klaus Fiedler, *Conflicted Power in Malawian Christianity*, Mzuzu: Mzuni Press, 2016, pp. 160-177.

[30] Wayne Grudem, *Systematic Theology: An Introduction to Biblical Doctrine*, Leicester: InterVarsity, 1994, pp. 458-459.

should think that there are any second-class citizens in the church. If we are equal in God's image, then certainly men and women are equally important to God and equally valuable to him.[31] Equality before God is further emphasized in the new covenant church in the ceremony of baptism. At Pentecost both men and women who believed were baptized: "those who received his word were baptized, and there were added that day about three thousand souls" (Acts 2:41). This is significant because in the old covenant, the sign of membership of God's people was circumcision, which was given only to men. The new sign of membership of God's people, the sign of baptism, given to both men and women, is further evidence that both should be seen as fully and equally members of the people of God.

There is reason to claim that Gal 3:28 supports an egalitarianism of function in the church. It does plainly teach an egalitarianism of privilege in the covenantal union of believers in Christ. As Christians, we are encouraged from the text to live in communion, which we can define as people or groups of people holding or being held together despite or in their differences. This I argue is the basis of inclusive theology. Paul's teaching is a challenge to CCAP Zambia's leadership to create adequate space for the ordained ministry for women. Women have found comfort and strength through their faith in Christ, while at the same time they have also experienced interpretations and practices that are male dominated and suppressive. They have experienced their embodiment as something negative in many Christian traditions due to the dualistic worldview of the western theology that places soul over body and male over female. The nature and extent of our equality is at

---

[31] This equality is an amazing and wonderful element of the Christian faith and sets Christianity apart from almost all religions and societies and cultures. The true dignity of godly manhood and womanhood can be fully realized only in obedience to God's redeeming wisdom as found in scripture. Cf. Wayne Grudem, *Systematic Theology: An Introduction to Biblical Doctrine,* Leicester: InterVarsity, 1994, p. 459.

the heart of the controversy. The solution in the case of gender therefore depends on the extent to which these political, cultural and theological paradigms are challenged. It is now crucial to remember that, in spite of the apparent misogyny that underpins the Christian religion, it offered women a revolution, as long as they subscribed to its precepts. St. Paul wrote: "There is neither Jew nor Greek, there is neither male nor female; for ye are all one in Christ Jesus"(Gal 3:28). The early church offered brotherhood to all men and women, in a manner unknown in the world of late antiquity. Although it considered women socially subject to the male, it granted them an identical immortal soul. Women were therefore equal in religion as long as the Christian code was accepted, and that entailed accepting its view of sex and childbirth.[32]

An examination of this verse in its contexts shows that it is speaking of equality of male and female in our worth to God and our standing before God. This is indeed an insight of great significance, which represents a substantial step forward in Christian understanding of man and woman before God. There is an approach which sees in this passage a contradiction with "lesser" or "lower" views of male/female relationships which are supposed to exist elsewhere in Paul's writings. But Galatians 3:28 is not contradicting what is found in those other passages.[33]

An interpretation of Galatians 3:28 in its immediate context must begin by carefully considering lexical and phraseological questions. First, we must consider the meaning of **ouk eni** in verse 28a. **Ouk eni** is translated as a mere negation of 'to be' giving the statement 'there is no Jew or Greek.' This is then usually supplemented by the adverbial phrase 'no longer.' But this last statement is unsupported in Greek text and such a reading also shifts the focus of sustained attention everywhere else, to

---

[32] Ibid, pp. 458-459.

[33] Ward Powers, *The Ministry of Women in the Church*, Adelaide: SPCKA, 1996, p. 116.

the categories being negated. A better rendering should take **ouk eni** as a shortened form of **ouk enesti**, yielding the emphatic negation 'it is not possible to be...' ('to be' must be supplied here but this is quite normal for Paul). This construal can then take an implicit subject emphasis for that verb, and in context this links up in turn with the baptized of verse 27, thereby retaining the context's broader emphasis on the Galatian Christians. Hence these famous negations can be translated '*It is not possible for you to be a Jew or a Greek, it is not possible for you to be a slave or freeman, it is not possible for you to be a man or woman,*' rather a stronger and more personal set of negations. What, however, is the origin of the three antitheses that Paul negates here so firmly? At this point we have to establish the meaning of the Binary Couplets in Verse 28a.[34]

These three binary oppositions in Galatians 3:28a summarize a Hellenistic ideology concerning human society attested at length in, for example, Aristotle's *Politics,* but found vestigially in other places as well, including Jewish prayers. The third couplet in Paul's citation also contains a tell-tale divergence. However, it negates not 'male or female', (or even ' man or woman') but 'masculine and feminine.' So, Paul seems to have Adamic or created humanity here; a broader canvas indeed. But on what is this striking negation, essentially of the present cosmos, grounded? At this point we are forced to appeal to the statements that immediately precede V.28a in V.27: *osoi (gar) eis christen ebaptisthete, Christon evedusasthe.*[35]

Verse 27 begins to supply a positive warrant for the negation of the foregoing categories using the two "whole body" metaphors of immersion and re-clothing drawn from the ritual of baptism. These also employ the metaphor of spatial movement to suggest something: the baptized have moved, as into water, into Christ, and have also been

---

[34] Ibid, p. 61.

[35] Ibid, p. 62.

clothed in Christ. This movement also seems to denote a total or comprehensive change because it grounds the negation of the cosmic categories that follows immediately. But in order to grasp this negation fully, the analysis must be broadened a little further.[36]

There is need to understand parallelism and the notion of 'oneness.' At this stage it is helpful to note an important structural feature in the subsection that generates vital interpretative leverage, namely a striking parallelism between vv.26 and 28 that neatly brackets our particular text and its initial warrant in v.27, and this is a common device in Paul. The first of these brackets in v.26 states that 'in Christ' the Galatians are 'sons of God'; something clearly derived from Christ's sonship that Paul gives more details of in 4:1-10. The parallel statement in v.28b complements this claim with the important motif of 'one-ness' (*eis*). It is in fact more likely that the use of 'one' here by Paul, paralleling as it does the phrase 'sons of God', means nothing more than '*one and the same*', so it is not undergirding a part–whole analogy at all. At this point we can dispense with a whole raft of interpretations that sail off into the realms of androgyny. These judgments are based on a demonstrable misreading of the text, which suggests and affirms clearly that the state inhabited by Galatian Christians is a uniform but personal and pluralized condition.[37] It is then argued that the translation within which Paul's argument appears a little more clearly would be:

> *For all of you are, by means of the faithful one, sons of God in Christ Jesus. For you have been immersed into Christ; you have been clothed in Christ.*
>
> *It is not possible, for you, to be a Jew or a Greek;*

---

[36] Douglas A. Campbell, "The Logic of Eschatology; The Implication of Paul's Gospel for Gender as Suggested by Galatians 3:28a in Context," in Douglas A. Campbell (ed), *Gospel and Gender: A Trinitarian Engagement with being Male and Female in Christ*, New York: T&T Clark, 2003, pp. 58-81, esp. pp. 63.

[37] Ibid, pp. 63-64.

> *It is not possible to be a slave or freeperson;*
> *It is not possible to be 'male and female';*
> *For all of you are one and the same in Christ Jesus.*

In short, we can say that Galatians 3:28 in context is a radical, abolitionist, and therefore political and liberating text. In the final analysis we must interpret Gal 3:28 in context in terms of what it is attempting to say and not in terms of what it does not attempt to address.[38] I therefore argue that those who are reading Galatians 3:28 not as a responsive, inclusive and liberating text are reading it wrongly. This was the theology of Paul to the Galatian Christians. Other texts that are not liberatingly interpreted need to be mirrored in the spirit of Paul advocating equality.

According to the Bible, gender differentiation is created and accepted. The apparent marginalization of women folk in society based on their feminine gender is not inherent in creation. Looking at the Pauline corpus, particularly Gal 3:28, Paul also recognizes gender differences. There is no distinction between "male and female." Gal 3:28 is the first occurrence of a text openly propagating the abolition of sex distinctions.[39] But abolishing sex distinction is not the same as abolishing gender roles. What lies behind Paul's views here is the fact that there was discrimination in the sexes. This discrimination is what Paul seeks to abolish in the Church. In other words, "Paul is speaking of equal privileges between men and women."[40] It is this parity that Henderson of the Free Church of Scotland fought for when he was the president of the Fellowship of Equal Service in the Church. His aim was to remove the barriers to the eligibility of women for the ministry and the eldership

---

[38] Ibid, p. 81.

[39] Hilary Mijoga, "Gender Differentiation in the Bible: Created and Recognized," in Jonathan Nkhoma, *Significance of the Dead Sea Scrolls and other Essays*, Mzuzu: Mzuni Press, 2013, pp. 176-198, esp. pp. 191-198.

[40] Ibid, pp. 191-198.

and he appealed for the admission of women to eldership.[41] The Church in Zambia needs men like Henderson to rise to the occasion and promote inclusiveness and participation as a strategy in realizing potential in women.

I also agree as far as the theological discourse on the issue of women's equality with men and even ordination is concerned. To this effect, I affirm the idea that women "have full title to the order of Christian ministry as God shall call them."[42] This is because of the complementarities of sexuality in both.

> Because God made 'man' male and female, in the natural realm men are fathers and brothers, while women are mothers and sisters. So, it must be in the spiritual realm. And when it is, then, and only then, will the church be truly the family of God.[43]

In Gal 3:28 Paul provides a breakthrough.[44] It is this breakthrough which CCAP Zambia should maximize by allowing women to take up influential decision-making leadership positions.

This text, Gal 3:28, is the Magna Charta for equality. The key to its interpretation may be the inclusion of slave and free. Paul's letters clearly show that he accepted slavery, though he never commended it. Though a social reality, this reality cannot be seen as good and commendable and must therefore be challenged from the systematic statement of Paul. The same reasoning should be applied to the statement that there is neither male nor female. Rachel NyaGondwe

---

[41] See Jurgens Johannes van Wyk, *The Historical Development of the Offices according to the Presbyterian Tradition of Scotland,* Zomba: Kachere, 2004 for a detailed discussion on the historical development of the offices according to the Presbyterian Tradition of Scotland, Chap 5, pp. 106-128.

[42] Robert Jewett, "The Sexual Liberation of the Apostle Paul," *Journal of the American Academy of Religion*, no. 47, 1979, pp. 53-87.

[43] Ibid.

[44] Ibid.

Fiedler observes that "just as much as slaves in their days were right in reading Gal 3:28 as a powerful critique of existing conditions, so women in the nineteenths century were, and today are, right in reading the same verse as a powerful critique of existing conditions in church and society."[45]

If one follows the foregoing reasoning, Galatians 3:28 falls easily into place.[46] Paul's highest insight into the full Christian relation between men and women is found in this verse. Accordingly, those churches that hold this interpretation are appointing women as ministers and priests, in accordance with the principle of equality that they see set out by Paul in Galatians 3:28. This text is a hermeneutical key by which we may go through any door we choose.[47] On the one hand then we note the considerable importance which is attached to the implications of this verse by those who regard it as establishing a basis for complete equality between the sexes, including in particular in the sphere of ministry: Jewett asserts that after Galatians 3:28 "there is nothing more to be said: Paul's word in his epistle of Christian liberty is the last word."[48] He contends that Galatians 3:28 is the necessary theological starting place for any discussion on the role of women in the church. Paul excludes all discrimination against Gentiles, slaves or women. Jewett concludes from this verse that in the life of the church the

---

[45] Rachel NyaGondwe Fiedler et al, *African Feminist Hermeneutics: An Evangelical Reflection*, Mzuzu: Mzuni Press, 2016, p. 112.

[46] Klaus Fiedler, "Gender Equality in the New Testament: The Case of St Paul," in Klaus Fiedler, *Conflicted Power in Malawian Christianity*, Mzuzu: Mzuni Press, 2016, pp. 160-177.

[47] Snodgrass Klyne R, "Galatians 3:28: Conundrum or Solution?" in Mickelsen, *Women*, 1987, pp. 161-167.

[48] See for example, Chapter Five, "Pauline Contradictions and Biblical Inspiration" in Virginia Mollenkott, *Women, Men, and the Bible*, Nashville: Abingdon, 1977, pp. 142-149;

oneness of the body of Christ must always be emphasized. Paul believes that gender distinctions cease in Christ (Gal 3:28).[49]

This discussion reveals that as the church was growing in membership in Galatia, many cultural and traditional problems crept into it because those who were converted to the church brought into it their former practices and beliefs, one of which was gender inequality, with which Paul wrestles in Gal 3:28.

Women in some Passages of the Pauline Letters

Interpretations of 1 Corinthians 11:2-16

1 Corinthians should be understood not only through the male-female segregation, but also through the male and female attire in the Greco-Roman world.[50] The Christian gospel called for an end to the segregation that so often barred one sex or the other from full religious participation. The cults of Mithras, Hercules and Orpheus were not ordinarily open to women. Conversely, Julius Caesar divorced his wife when she permitted a man to enter the house during the rites of Bona Dea. Even within the same Cult a given festival might admit only one sex.[51] This exclusivity was defended fiercely. For example, King Bathos insisted to attend the all-female rite of the Thesmophoria, the women allowed him but they seized the sacrificial knives and removed from the king's body the organ that distinguished him as male, and thereafter proceeded with the ceremony. Also, Pentheus dressed as a woman to spy upon an all-female celebration of the rites of Dionysos. Two statues of the god stood in the market place at Corinth and were said to have

---

[49] Bernadette J. Brooten, "Early Christian Women and their Cultural Context: Issues of Method in Historical Reconstruction," in Adela Y. Collins, (ed), *Feminist Perspectives on Biblical Scholarship*, Society of Biblical Literature, Chico: Scholars, 1985, pp. 65-92, esp. p. 85.

[50] Catherine Kroeger, "The Apostle Paul and the Greco-Roman World Cults of Women," *JETS*, (Paul and the Cults of Women), March 1987, pp. 25-38 [32-38].

[51] Ibid, p. 32.

been carved from the very tree hence the women pulled this peeping Tom to his death.[52]

On one hand, female worshippers of Dionysos were known as *maenads*, meaning 'mad ones.' This term did not apply to men. It was usually women who were smitten by the god's *mania*. These women, who seldom saw the world that lay outside their own front door, hailed him as their liberator, *Lusios*. Women in the NT era, though in a somewhat more restricted fashion, still knew this god's frenzy and rejoiced in his liberating *mania*.[53] The same religious madness or *mania* was said to be present in the Corinthian congregation, that swayed the Christians (1Cor 12:1-2). An uninformed person who walked into their ecstatic service would certainly look upon the excesses as religiously inspired madness (1Cor 14:23). It is within this context that we should seek to understand Paul's directives to the Corinthians.[54]

On the other hand, headgear was expedient for Jewish women, among whom properly bound hair and veiling was obligatory unless they wished for a divorce. Upper-class Roman women might go uncovered, but the lower-class women in the provinces usually wore a veil. The women of Paul's home town Tarsus were routinely veiled. Since the congregation at Corinth met next door to the Synagogue and was composed of both Jewish and Gentile women, universal veiling of women would certainly cause the least offence.[55]

The veiling issue had other ramifications as well. A careful reading of 1Cor 11 demonstrates that the instruction is equally explicit about proper attire and hairstyle for men. This was due to sex reversal practiced in some of the cults, most commonly manifested in clothing

---

[52] Ibid, p. 32.

[53] Ibid, p. 34.

[54] Ibid, p. 34.

[55] Ibid, p. 37.

exchange. Such sex reversal was a specific distinctive of the Dionysian cult and by the second century AD was considered to be indispensable to the religion. Men wore veils and long hair as a sign of their dedication to the god, while women used the unveiling and the shorn hair to indicate their devotion. Men masqueraded as women, and in a rare vase painting from Corinth a woman is dressed in Satyr pants equipped with the male organ. She dances before Dionysos, a deity who had been raised as a girl and was himself called male-female and "Sham-man." The sex exchange that characterized the cults of Artemis of Ephesus was more grisly.[56] Artemis was the goddess of hunting, agriculture, wild nature, and chastity. The story of Sipriotes, a young boy who saw the goddess bathing and whom Artemis turned into a girl (Atsma) confirms what this goddess was thought to be capable of doing.[57]

By contrast Paul asked Christians to maintain their own identity in a clear differentiation of the sexes in garments, hairstyle and self-expression (1Cor 11:2-16). The veil was used as a symbol of commitment, while a strongly egalitarian statement reminds both men and women that neither is independent of the other and that both sexes find their origin in God. In its context, 1Cor 11:11-12 calls for an end to segregated religion based upon sex hostility, exclusivity, and a desire to claim an inside track of spiritual knowledge. This is the same context of silence theology in 1Cor 14:34-35. Kroeger notes that these decrees take on new meaning if Paul is speaking out against vestigial pagan practices in a newly converted congregation.[58] Pauline mandates deserve a great deal of scrutiny and must be examined not only in the light of their context in the NT writings, but also against a background of contemporary attitudes and practice. This not only calls for knowing

---

[56] Ibid, p. 37, The word grisly means extremely unpleasant and frightening usually connected with death and violence.

[57] Atsma, Aaron 2009, http/theo.com/hympos/Artemis.htm [23.2.21].

[58] Ibid, p. 37.

far more about the religions of ancient women but also, we must use literary evidence, archeological monuments, coins, papyri and art historic materials such as vases and wall paintings. If we are to deal with the hard sayings on women in the Pauline corpus, it should be done with integrity.[59]

In 1 Corinthians 11:2-16, Paul discusses the appropriate headdress for men and women during the worship service. The basic rule for church order that Paul gives in this passage is that in worship services men should leave their heads uncovered, while women should cover their heads.[60] Bacchiocchi notes that when Paul speaks of 'head' in this passage he actually talks about 'functional headship or order of hierarchy.' He observes that the hierarchical distinctions are functional and not ontological, because they have to do with roles and not with essential worth or dignity of being.[61] Bacchiocchi emphatically states that the veiling of the head by women was a predominant Jewish custom. He argues that while the principle of head dress may be permanent in its application, it will vary in different cultures.[62] However, Paul was demanding Corinthian Christian women and men to follow Jewish custom in regard to headgear and hairstyle and that the custom of head covering by women was common in Corinth because Paul shows that Christian churches practiced this custom.[63] This is patently a very rabbinic passage. Paul had not yet emancipated himself from the thought patterns of his Jewish-Pharisaic training. However, women did not agree with Paul. It was presumably their refusing to wear the sign

---

[59] Ibid, p. 38.

[60] Samuele Bacchiocchi, *Women in the Church: A Biblical Study on the Role of Women in the Church,* Berrien Springs: Biblical Perspectives, 1987, p. 126.

[61] Ibid.

[62] Ibid, p. 131.

[63] Hans Conzelman, *A Commentary on the First Epistle to the Corinthians,* Hermeneia, Philadelphia: Fortress, 1975, p. 185.

of submission that caused Paul to write on the subject and to formulate a theology of headship as theoretical support for the practice of veiling. Whether the Corinthian women finally accepted either Paul's subordinationist theology or his command that they be veiled we do not know.[64]

The word 'head' as used in this context is evidently used in a transferred sense. In the Old Testament, the Hebrew ראש (rosh) translated as 'head' may refer to the ruler of a community as in Judges 10:18. This use, though it was adopted in Greek-speaking Judaism, was not a native meaning of the Greek word. In Greek usage, the word may apply to the outstanding and determining part of a whole, but also to origin. In this sense, the word is used theologically. Therefore, Paul does not say that man is the $κυριος$ (kurios) 'lord' of the woman but that he is the origin of her being. Barrett believes that Paul is directly dependent on Genesis 2:18-23 where it is stated that woman was created in order to provide a helper suited to Adam, and that Eve was created by the removal of a rib from Adam's body. He further observes that Paul is indeed partly influenced by this verse when in 1Cor 11, after writing that man is the image and glory of God, he says that woman is the glory of man, not his image, for she too shares the image of God, and is not more remote from God than is man.[65]

What Paul wants the Corinthians to realize is, first of all, the nature of headship. In Greek as in English, 'head' refers both to that part of the anatomy and also to the concept of the one in a given organizational hierarchy who has a role of leadership in relation to another or others.

---

[64] Bernadette J. Brooten, "Early Christian Women and their Cultural Context: Issues of Method in Historical Reconstruction," Adela Y. Collins (ed), *Feminist Perspectives on Biblical Scholarship,* Society of Biblical Literature, Chico: Scholars, 1985, pp. 72-85.

[65] C.K. Barrett, *First Epistle to the Corinthians,* 2nd ed., London: Adam and Charles Black, 1971, pp. 248-249.

In this passage Paul utilizes the range of meaning possessed by this word *'kephale' in Greek*. The meaning in Paul's use of it is the one who has a role of leadership. Thus, Christ has the leadership role for every man, and the man has the leadership role for his wife, and God has this role for Jesus Christ. But the question of relationship of man and woman to Christ is covered in what Paul wrote in Galatians 3:28, where he shows that in Christ Jesus male and female are equal.[66] Also, another challenging issue the apostle Paul tackles is the *importance of hierarchy* (vv. 3 and 7-9). Paul states that, "The head of every man is Christ, the head of a woman is her husband, and the head of Christ is God" (v.3). Some New Testament scholars like Robin Scroggs prefer using the word "source" for the Greek word *kephale* which is here translated as "head." But Richardson uses the word in terms of "authority," not source as in Phil 1:21-22; 5:22-23; and Col 1:18.[67] Thus, the behaviour of a woman who wishes to violate the accepted social practices by defying the distinctions of gender is unacceptable for a Christian.[68] Therefore, the Corinthian woman was not supposed to show her authority by having her head uncovered, especially when this represented heretical practices.

---

[66] Ward Powers, *The Ministry of Women in the Church: Which way forward?* Adelaide: SPCKA, 1996, pp. 71-72.

[67] Richardson points out that a thorough study of the use of *kephale* was made by Joseph A. Fitzmyer, "Another Look at *kephale* in 1 Corinthians 11:3," *New Testament Studies* 35, 1998, pp. 503-511. Fitzmyer makes a strong case for the meaning "head" instead of "source" (see esp. 510). See also A.C. Perriman, "The Head of a Woman: The Meaning of *kephale* in 1 Corinthians 11:3," *Journal of Theological Studies*, 45, 1994, pp. 602-622. We should observe, however, a point that is not obvious in an English translation: Where Paul writes that the 'husband' is head, he does not use the definite article ('head', not 'the head'), what does this mean? Simply this: man is not the absolute head of the wife.

[68] Larry Richardson, "How does a Woman Prophesy and Keep Silence at the same Time? (1 Corinthians 11 and 14)," in Nancy Vyhmeister (ed), *Women in Ministry,* Berrien Springs: Andrews University Press, 1998.

Paul's instruction to the Corinthian Church on headdress is attributed to cultural practices prevalent then. To understand what Paul says in this passage demands knowledge of prevailing ancient customs. It was proper in the Roman Empire for a respectable woman to veil herself in public.[69] This may mean that there were some women who did not respect themselves and never veiled themselves as the custom demanded and this was quite strange. This chapter deals with conduct at divine worship. Conzelman suggests that Paul was demanding that the Corinthian Christian women and Christian men follow the Jewish custom in regard to headgear and hairstyle. He further argues that the custom was universal because Paul shows that Christian churches practiced this custom. He explains how strict this custom was. For example, for a Jewess to go out with her head uncovered was a disgrace and grounds for divorce.[70] According to Jewish custom a bride went bareheaded until her marriage, as a symbol of her freedom, because when married, she wore a veil as a sign that she was under the authority of her husband.[71] It is noted by Tertullian that Jewish women could be recognized on the streets of North Africa by the veils they wore on their heads.[72]

In complement to this, Tarsus, the home city of Paul, was noted for its strict adherence to this rule of propriety. The veil covered the head from view, but not the face, and was at once a symbol of subordination to the male and of the respect a woman deserved. Gundry agrees with Hooker that married women were culturally demanded to veil their

---

[69] Robert Gundry, *A Survey of the New Testament,* Grand Rapids: Zondervan, 1981, pp. 266-267.

[70] Hans Conzelman, *A Commentary on the First Epistle to the Corinthians,* Hermeneia, Philadelphia: Fortress, 1975, pp. 182, 185.

[71] M.D. Hooker, "Authority on her Head: An Examination of 1 Corinthians 11: 10," *New Testament Studies* 10, 1964, p. 413.

[72] Tertullian, *De Corona 4, The Ante-Nicene Fathers,* Alexander Roberts and James Donaldson (eds), Grand Rapids, vol. 3, 1973, p. 95.

heads in order to respect their husbands and indeed respect themselves. He observes that Christians at Corinth, however, were following the custom of some unrespectable Greek women who left their heads uncovered when they worshipped. And so, he defends Paul that this is the reason why he vehemently says that it is disgraceful for Christian women to prophesy in church services with unveiled heads or alternatively with long hair uncovered.[73] This is in line with verse 15 which states 'but if a woman has long hair, it is a glory to her; for her hair is given to her for a covering.

There is need to establish the possible reason that prompted Paul to remind the Corinthian Christians on the tradition of head gear. Keener observes that even though the custom of head covering was common in those days, upper-class women did not comply and were eager to show off their fashionable hairstyles and, therefore, did not practice it. He argues that in this case Paul had to address a clash of culture in the church between upper-class fashion and lower-class concern that sexual propriety was being violated.[74]

While Paul gives instruction on the issue of proper decorum during worship, he allows women to pray and prophesy while their heads are covered or veiled. Robertson and Plummer say that prophesying means public teaching, admonishing or comforting; delivering God's message to the congregation. They point out that it is arbitrary today to say that a man is to lead in full public worship while a woman should only lead in mission services or family prayers, and that in public worship women were not to speak at all. They suggest that women may have argued that, if the Spirit moved them to speak, they needed to. This could not be possible if their faces were veiled. They suggest that in such cases

---

[73] Robert Gundry, *A Survey of the New Testament,* Grand Rapids: Zondervan, 1981, pp. 266-267.

[74] Craig S. Keener, *The IVP Bible Backgrounds Commentary- New Testament,* Downers Grove, Illinois: InterVarsity, 1993, p. 475.

the Apostle Paul advises that they must speak while their faces are veiled according to culture so that they don't outrage propriety by coming to public worship unveiled because of the mere possibility that the Spirit may compel them to speak.[75]

According to Richards, a study of 1 Corinthians 14:34-35 comparing it with 1Cor 11 suggests that these were not Paul's genuine words but interpolations. But he maintains that Paul is the author of the words.[76] He observes that in order for one to do justice to the above text, one should study it in the context of the previous chapter 1Cor 11:2-17. In this text "Paul deals with the problem of Corinthian women attending worship services dressed in an unconventional manner with their heads uncovered."[77] Thus, in chapter 11, justice is done to both chapters 11 and 14 for both men and women as far as their role in the church is concerned. Therefore, chapter 11 should be viewed as a positive background chapter, not only to chapter 14, but to the entire epistle to the Corinthians.

He attributes this to a Gnostic heretical teaching background that flamed the need to reprimand the Corinthian Church the way Paul did. According to this teaching, this heresy was based on the belief that "knowledge" was the basis for salvation. It was not based on God's grace centred on the Cross.[78] A Gnostic believed that he/she was part of the divine. This knowledge was salvation for the Gnostic. Thus, a Gnostic was a person who was spiritual from all eternity. Hence, to a

---

[75] Archibald Robertson and Alfred Plummer, *First Epistle of St. Paul to the Corinthians, The International Critical Commentary*, Edinburgh: T&T Clark, 1963, p. 230.

[76] W. Larry Richards, "How Does a Woman Prophesy and Keep Silence at the Same Time? (1 Corinthians 11 and 14)," in Nancy Vyhmeister (ed), *Women in Ministry*, Berrien Springs: Andrews University Press, 1998, p. 313.

[77] Ibid, p. 313.

[78] Ibid, p. 315.

Gnostic, everything connected to the material world was considered evil.[79]

Also, a Gnostic believed that the creation of male and female, which was a wholesome and natural feature of a good God's creation (Gen 1:27, 31), was a by-product of an inferior development within the cosmos, ascribed to an evil God. Accordingly, to a Gnostic, the physical being was of no value. The physical hindered the Gnostic realizing his/her true spiritual (immortal) identity. Hence, to the Gnostic, gender distinctions should be ignored since male and female belong to the fallen world. Therefore, as a female, a Gnostic was not different from the Gnostic male; they both had the same divine spark.[80]

This Gnostic teaching influenced some women in the Corinthian Church to think that, in reality, only the spiritual aspects were important. They challenged the conventional worship customs. In this way, a Gnostic believed that a woman who wore a veil and kept her hair long acknowledged what the Gnostics denied. Accordingly, the respect that was shown for angels (v.10) was pure nonsense of following conventional practices. Therefore, Gnostic women behaved in such a way that they considered themselves equal or superior to angels. This is why "Gnostic Christians" in Corinth, who behaved in such an audacious manner, were asked by Paul if they thought they were superior to the Lord (1Cor 10:22).[81]

---

[79] Ibid.

[80] Ibid.

[81] Ibid, p. 316. See: Robin Scroggs, "Paul and the Eschatological Woman," *Journal of the American Academy of Religion* 40, 1972, p. 285. "Gnostic Christianity also seems to have shared some of the same insights with Paul, but in general there is one critical difference between them. Both agree on eliminating value judgments of man over against woman. The Gnostics seem to have wanted to go further, however, to obliterate all distinctions between the sexes. Paul is, passionate in keeping the reality of the distinctions; he just will not suffer any value judgment to be drawn on the basis of distinctions. "

Paul begins and ends his discourse with the importance of tradition (verses 2, 16) in his expression, "holding on to tradition." He appeals to the tradition of all the churches in this expression (v.2). Tradition is something that is handed down from one generation to another. But this can be a cultural tradition (see Mt 15:2-6) or even a tradition contrary to the will of God (see Mk 7:8). Also, it may be an entirely good tradition as in this passage expressed by Paul. Therefore, Paul wrote that "We have no other practice nor do the churches of God" (v.16). He wanted everything to be done to the glory of God (10:31).[82]

Another point to note in the context of 1 Corinthians 11 is the use of the word "wife" which is here used in Greek as *gune*. Here, *gune* is under the authority of her husband (*aner*). She is not under the subordination of any other man in the church or society in general. Consequently, Paul is not putting the woman down, but is countering a Gnostic position.[83]

Also, *the matter of honour* (vv. 4-6) is Paul's other position. When Paul says that "every man who prays or prophesies with his head covered dishonours his head" (v.4), he uses the word "head" in two ways. The first usage refers to man's physical head while the second refers probably to his spiritual Head (Christ). In this way, when a man prays with his head covered (physical head), he displays dishonour toward Christ (his spiritual Head). Paul also says the same for a woman. A woman who prays or prophesies in public worship with her head uncovered also dishonours her head. This is the same as having her hair completely cut or shaved (v.5). Since this is shameful, a woman should therefore have her head properly covered, either with long hair or with a veil when praying and prophesying (v.6). A woman who uncovered or shaved her hair was either known as loose in morals or as sexually

---

[82] W. Larry Richards, "How Does a Woman Prophesy and Keep Silence at the Same Time? (1 Corinthians 11 and 14)," in Nancy Vyhmeister (ed), *Women in Ministry*, Berrien Springs: Andrews University, 1998, p. 318.

[83] Ibid, p. 323.

promiscuous. Therefore, what is traditionally said for a man when praying and prophesying is also said for a woman when performing the same task. The text does not suggest that women should not preach.

It is argued that women were not allowed to pray and prophesy in public but were allowed to do so in private. However, there is little reason for believing that the praying and prophesying mentioned in verse 5 was to be done privately alone at home. Paul saw prophecy as a gift for public use.[84] Moreover, it is hard to believe that Paul would prohibit women from praying with their heads uncovered in the privacy of their homes. By the same token, it is hardly conceivable that Paul would forbid a man to pray with his head covered when alone outdoors or in the cold weather. The solution to the ambiguity in Paul's text is that gender distinctions are no longer there in Christ.[85]

Finally, we may understand Paul, in 1 Corinthians 11:4-16, to be reasoning with the Corinthians as to the principle of propriety and religious decorum in terms of the particular customs of the day. It seems evident that custom has considered an uncovered head as proper for a man but improper for a woman. Proceeding, then, on the assumption that Paul is here dealing with the application of a principle to the custom of the country and the times, we can safely take his words theologically without concluding that his specific application of the principle then requires the same specific application today.[86]

---

[84] Samuele Bacchiocchi, *Women in the Church: A Biblical Study on the Role of Women in the Church*, Berrien Springs: Biblical Perspectives, 1987, p. 165.

[85] Bernadette J. Brooten, "Early Christian Women and Their Cultural Context: Issues of Method in Historical Reconstruction," in Adela Y. Collins (ed), *Feminist Perspectives on Biblical Scholarship: Society of Biblical Literature*, Chico: Scholars, 1985, pp. 65-92, esp. 86.

[86] Francis D. Nichol (ed), *Seventh-day Adventist Bible Commentary*, Vol. 6, Hagerstown: Review and Herald Publishing Association, 1957, p. 754. It also provides an example from the Old Testament: Moses was asked by the Lord to remove his shoes before him (Exod. 3: 5) because "It was evidently the custom

This chapter has words of utmost importance which are at the centre of understanding the role of women in the church. In 1Cor 11:2, Paul commends Corinthian Christians for keeping the traditions that he had taught them before and wanted to teach them more of these traditions, probably because of a strange practice that had transpired which Paul had heard about. The word that Paul uses and has been translated 'traditions' is παραδοσεις (paradoseis) from the noun παραδο-σις (paradosis).This word basically means 'handing down or over' in the sense of the following: (1) betrayal, arrest, (2) tradition, of teachings, commandments, narratives, (3) of the tradition preserved by the scribes and Pharisees.[87] In the English language the word 'tradition' means belief, principle or way of acting which people in a particular society or group have continued to follow for a long time.[88] The passage under study does not manifest any type of strife or any unlawful undertaking. Therefore, the first meaning does not apply in this case because no arrests or betrayals took place. Paul took time to teach the Corinthian congregation tradition which may be 'teachings', or 'commandments' in terms of what the church was supposed to follow during worship times. Since members of this church came from Jewish and Greek backgrounds it is possible that Paul taught this church acceptable and practical tradition from the two backgrounds to preserve order.

All the quoted theologians assume that Paul wanted the women, at least in Corinth, to cover their head (at least in prayer), though they may differ on the issue of applicability.

---

in that area of the world to show respect for holy places by removing the shoes. The principle of proper reverence still stands inviolate, but the practice of expressing such reverence may vary greatly with countries and times."

[87] William F. Arndt, Wilbur F. Gingrich, *A Greek - English Lexicon of the New Testament and other Early Christian Literature,* Fourth Revised and augmented edition, Chicago: The University of Chicago Press, 1952, p. 621.

[88] *Cambridge Advanced Learner's Dictionary*, Third edition, New York: Cambridge University Press, 2008.

This is not shared by Joan Taylor, who argues that Paul gave women authority (*exousia*)[89] over their own heads (v.10), to cover the head or not. She does not agree with the majority opinion that *exousia, here alone* in the NT, means exactly the opposite, namely that women must subject to another authority and have none of their own. She argues that there is nothing in the source material from the classical world that would indicate that a veil or other form of head/body covering indicated female inferiority or subjection to men. The practice of modest women covering the upper body with a mantle, the *himation* or *pollium,* was not uniform throughout antiquity. It was distinctive in certain parts of the ancient world as feminine attire for married free women (not for unmarried girls, artisan women or slave women who were not expected to have much modesty) in public space, probably including Tarsus. However, in regard to Roman Corinth, respectable women could be seen in public without a head-covering. It was not standard dress. This comes through in the presentation of certain 'model' women whom all women should emulate in the Greco-Roman world. Taylor observes that such ideals are clearly relevant in the discussion of 1 Corinthians 11:2-16. Therefore, covering up was an ideal to which virtuous (generally elite, wealthy) women could aspire. Covering the head was distinctively feminine in terms of dress only insofar as it represented the ideal of modesty appropriate to a virtuous woman.[90]

The issue is made even more perplexing when consideration of what was appropriate for Jewish men is brought into the picture. In view of 1 Corinthians 11:2-16, the reference is apparently androcentric, in alluding to the practice of Christian men versus the practice of Jewish

---

[89] This has led to the translation of *exousia* as "a piece of cloth" (Kanthu ku mutu) in the Buku Loyera translation.

[90] Joan E. Taylor, "The Woman ought to have Control over her Head because of the Angels (1 Corinthians 11:10)," in Douglas A. Campbell (ed), *Gospel and Gender: A Trinitarian Engagement with being Male and Female in Christ*, New York: T&T Clark, 2003, pp. 37-57, esp. pp. 49-57.

men. Christian men see with unveiled face the Lord's glory as a mirror (which they look into). They see therefore their own reflection without any covering. There is no reason to assume that Paul is promoting Jewish convention in Corinth, whether for men or for women. Paul does not advocate that women cover up in front of all men.[91]

It is Paul who 'genders' headgear in the specific context of prayer for the Corinthians, insisting that it is a tradition that he himself is passing on, appropriate to the 'communities of God' (1Cor 11:16). The evidence from Greco-Roman culture indicates that both men and women of high status would do so more commonly in public than men in certain areas to show their exceptional virtue by means of such modesty. If a woman was throwing off her head-covering during prophecy and prayer and arguing that a veil was a distinctive form of *feminine* attire that was irrelevant in view of Gal 3:28, it was because Paul himself had asserted that it was a distinctive form of feminine attire in one context only: that of prayer and prophecy. The issue for Paul seems to be about how it all looks to God when prayer and prophecy is taking place. This circumstance would apply in public or private worship: the focus is God, not other people. Paul does not advocate that women cover up in front of all men. The rest of Paul's rhetoric makes sense when this is borne in mind. No matter how well-meaning we may assume Paul's motives to have been in promoting honour, modesty and order in recognition of the presence of God and the angels, one can only wonder at how astonished the women of Corinth may have felt at his words, given the strength of the prophetic power with which a woman was animated. The woman's silence may itself speak volumes.[92]

Most Bible translations have suggested that Paul wanted the women in the church of Corinth to cover their heads. But possibly Paul told them exactly the opposite because the word *exousia* elsewhere in the New

---

[91] Ibid, pp. 49-57.
[92] Ibid, pp. 49-57.

Testament means *authority* and *power* (Matt 7:29; Matt 9:6; Matt 10:1; Matt 11:23 and John 1:12). In none of these verses has *exousia* been translated as "sign of authority," but just as *authority*. Why not translate it in the same way when a woman is involved: "Therefore the woman ought to have authority over her head," and therefore she can wear a hat, a turban, cut the hair short, curl it or straighten it, add braids to it or let it grow to her waist or tie it into a knot. This interpretation fits well with what we know for sure about Paul: He appreciated highly the women's work for the Gospel.[93] If this was Paul's view, how do we reconcile his earlier statements which seem to demand female submission, compulsory headgear? An answer would be a quotation. If Paul gave the direction that women should be left alone as far as headdress is concerned, the opposing view could have been quoted from the letter which he received and in which these questions were asked. Then Paul's own words would be vv. 2-3 and 10-16, and vv. 4-9 would be opinions he quotes and disapproves of. This cannot be the ultimate answer. But it is definitely a possible interpretation, with maybe less loose ends than other more common interpretations.[94]

I therefore argue that based on the Greek word *exousia*, it was not compulsory for women to put on headgear (*Duku* or *Chitambala cha ku mutu* in Tumbuka), nor was it a sign of submission, but by choice. Joan Taylor, Rachel Fiedler and I see this as a possible interpretation rather than other more common interpretations. I urge that CCAP Zambia should find room in their theology where such an interpretation could find its place. This will be in line with Paul's theology of inclusiveness and liberation of women in the church as reflected in Galatians 3:28.

So, it appears that as Paul writes to the Corinthian Church in chapter 11, he provides a series of brief rhetorical arguments, each of which relates

---

[93] Rachel NyaGondwe Fiedler et al, *African Feminist Hermeneutics: An Evangelical Reflection*, Mzuzu: Mzuni Press, 2016, pp. 113-114.

[94] Ibid, pp. 114.

directly to the culture he addresses. As noted above, Paul was addressing a mixed congregation whose membership had diverse cultural backgrounds. Women from Greek, Roman, and Jewish backgrounds practiced their cultures. Paul's arguments, therefore, cannot fit well in every culture today. It was the Corinthian women, not modern women, whom he wished to persuade to cover their heads. In this chapter, it appears the bone of contention is not the head covering per se but how women should present themselves as they prophesy and pray in the worship service in church. Paul is laying down the principle of decorum during worship services. This was an acceptable method of showing reverence to God during worship times according to their practice. The theological principle of reverence during worship times Paul laid down still continues in our time despite our diverse cultures. God can be revered differently by different cultures throughout the world. The veiling of women's heads and the unveiling of men's heads during worship services were suitable to the culture of the time as a way of showing reverence to God.

Therefore, Paul does not forbid women in this chapter from public participation or proclamation of God's message in church services. He does not advocate for their silence. He is wrestling with cultural issues to fit well with their religion according to their context. Tribes all over the world have diverse cultures and they worship God within the context of their acceptable cultures and God accepts them. In our time, depending, of course, on the locality, the practice that applied to women concerning head covering would be practiced by those whose culture allows it. This, of course, does not affect a woman's faith, salvation or position in church.

Interpretations of 1 Corinthians 14:34-35

This passage has kindled much debate in scholarly circles. It has been the subject of considerable controversy, as it appears to stand in obvious contrast to 1 Corinthians 11:5 where Paul says that women should pray and prophesy in the church. Again, this seems to contradict the manner in which Paul himself worked with women and commended them in Romans 16. Scholars give varied interpretations to this passage.

To have a better understanding of 1Cor 14:34-35, there is need to know not only the ceremonial cries of women but also feminine reaction to male animosity in the Greco-Roman world.[95] The noise that frequently attended women's participation was in marked contrast to the silence required of men. Their voices were raised in formal rites, the *Olylygia* at the moment when the sacrificial animal fell.[96] Kroeger argues that in Aeschylus' play, Etieocles finally agrees to allow the women to engage in the only rite he considers appropriate for them: the raising of the *Olylygia*. This is the Grecian custom and brings joy to their allies and death to their foes.[97] In ecstatic cults, such as those of Cybele and Dionysos, *the Olylygia* was an essential ingredient of the religious hubbub of the rites. Women were not above using these sacred shouts to drawn out what the men were saying, even in solemn assemblies.[98] Kroeger asserts that at the beginning of the first century Strabo protested that everyone agreed in regarding women as the prime movers in religion. Plutarch, writing in the early second century of the Christian era, said that even the female worshippers of Osiris engaged in shoutings and movements similar to those of women in the sway of Dionysian frenzy. Kroeger then argues that a plaque excavated from the sanctuary of Demeter at Corinth is dedicated to the sacred cries of women and reads *"Olylygos,"* evidence that the phenomenon was alive and well at Corinth. These ritual cries of women are still an integral part of many cultures and persist in certain rural areas of Greece even

---

[95] Catherine Kroeger, "The Apostle Paul and the Greco-Roman World Cults of Women" (Paul and the Cults of Women), March 1987, pp. 25-38, esp. p. 29.

[96] Ibid, p. 29.

[97] Ibid.

[98] Ibid, p. 29.

today.[99] This may explain Paul's request in 1Cor 14:34-35 for silence on the part of women during ecstatic services that involved *madness, glossolalia (speaking in tongues),* and *prophecy*, all three known to have been part of the Dionysian religion, which appealed so enormously to women. In a passage that calls for no noise without meaning (1Cor 14:9,11-13,28) and even meaningful utterance to be restricted to one at a time (vv 29-31), an injunction against the tumultuous cries of women is appropriate.[100]

Although the cultic activities of women were far better accepted in the Roman era than they had been in the classical Greek age, still there were efforts to curb their free practice of religion.[101] Both Greek and Roman society had tried to regulate and restrain female piety by brute force as well as by legislative measures. The Roman Senate took stern action against the Cult of Dionysos, largely because the adherents were principally women, and Cicero forbade women performing sacrifices at night. It may well be a law such as this that is referred to by Paul in 1Cor 14:35 requiring women to be under control of men.[102] If women turned to other forms of religious expression, it was often a direct reaction to male animosity.[103]

The passage occurs in the context of the discussion of how to maintain order in the worship assemblies. With reference to spiritual gifts in 1Cor 14 Bacchiocchi's opinion is that beginning with verse 26, Paul gives instructions on how speaking in tongues and prophesying should be regulated in the church, so that good order might prevail. In this context, he says, Paul turns to instruct women to observe silence in

---

[99] Ibid, p. 30.
[100] Ibid.
[101] Ibid.
[102] Ibid.
[103] Ibid.

assemblies because they are women.[104] He argues against those whose opinion is that women made disorderly speech. He asserts that, if the problem was disorderly speech, then it is difficult to see why Paul would single out women or wives when in the immediate context he speaks of the confusion created by people in general who were speaking simultaneously in tongues or as prophets. He further explains that if the problem had been one of disorder, as was the case with tongues or prophecy, then Paul would have simply prescribed order. He would not prescribe the silence of women since not everyone who was behaving in a disorderly way was a woman.[105]

The analysis of 1 Corinthians 14 that Bacchiocchi makes, manifests biased sentiments. The silence that Paul speaks about in verse 34 is the same silence that he enjoins on men in verses 28 and 29. When Bacchiocchi says that Paul instructs women to keep silence because they were created as women, it must be clarified that this was the case because women were far less trained in the Scriptures and public reasoning than men were,[106] not because of their gender as Bacchiocchi assumes. Informed listeners customarily asked questions during lectures, but it was considered rude for the ignorant to do so.[107] Arguing against a popular notion that Paul instructs women of Corinth only as a custom, Bacchiocchi says that Paul here lays down a rule to be followed in all the churches of the saints and not just in a given culture. His opinion is that it is unlikely that the problem of noisy women had arisen in all the churches of the saints to prompt Paul to make a prohibition, but that it is shameful for a woman to speak in the church because she

---

[104] Samuele Bacchiocchi, *Women in the Church: A Biblical Study on the Role of Women in the Church,* Berrien Springs: Biblical Perspectives, 1987, p. 165.

[105] Samuele Bacchiocchi, *Women in the Church*, p. 166.

[106] Craig S. Keener, *The IVP Bible Background Commentary, New Testament,* Downers Grove, Illinois: InterVarsity, 1993, p. 483.

[107] Ibid, p. 483.

is a woman.[108] Bacchiocchi takes the prohibition to apply to all women in all congregations at all times.

After his conversion to Christianity, Paul accepted the practice he found in the church he had just joined where women prophesied and prayed in church worship assemblies. However, he demanded that they do so with veiled heads as custom required. Reuther assumes, as other scholars do, that 1 Corinthians 14:34-35 is an interpolation from the next generation after Paul,[109] or a post-Pauline interpolation.[110] The words of Paul found in this passage are problematic. Their authorship is doubted and even imagining that the words belong to the Apostle Paul is difficult. Denis Duling explains that the external and internal problems of these verses have led some to believe that these verses were added much later by a scribe, since if these seemingly contradicting verses are removed, the text reads much more smoothly. He observes that these verses seem to contradict, not only the rest of the Bible, but even Paul himself in multiple places and in the very same letter as in 1Cor 11:5 and 12:4-11.[111] The other reason Duling gives for accepting that interpolation took place is that the writing style employed in these verses is utterly foreign to Paul's writing style. He argues that even the 'Law' appealed to, to justify silencing of women, does not exist anywhere in the Old Testament and that nowhere in the Old Testament does any law or command require that women 'subject themselves' by being 'silent' in an assembly or while in public. He also notes that if one reads verses 34-35 from the Corinthians and verses 36-38 as Paul's

---

[108] Ibid, p. 165.

[109] Rosemary Radford Ruether, *Women and Redemption: A Theological History,* Minneapolis: Fortress, 1998, p. 6

[110] William O. Walker Jr., "The Theology of Women's Place and the Paulinist Tradition," *Semeia* 28, 1983, p. 101.

[111] Denis C. Duling, *The New Testament: History, Literature, and Social Context,* Belmont: Thomson Woodsworth, 2003, p. 24.

response, the meaning becomes clear and totally conducive to the rest of Paul's letter. This interpolation sentiment is also echoed for 1Cor 14:33-36. Duling thinks that it is probably an interpolation by a Paulinist. There are two reasons he gives for considering this passage as an interpolation inserted by a later Paulinist. First, he observes that it interrupts the context because it does not easily agree with Paul's previous statements that women should prophesy in worship. Secondly, the passage also appeals to the Law in a rather un-Pauline way. It is believed that the passage might have come from the Pauline school in the early second century AD, about three generations later.[112]

A growing number of scholars argue that 1 Corinthians 14:34-35 are not the words of Paul, but that Paul is quoting the letter written to him from the church at Corinth. Kaiser says that these verses contradict everything Paul has instructed the Corinthians up until this point. He argues that there is no such 'law' in the Torah or the entire Old Testament that requires women to be silent. He further argues that there are other clues in the original manuscripts that support the view that Paul was quoting from the letter written to him by the Corinthian Church. There are two points he vehemently mentions to support his view. He argues that ancient Greek did not have punctuation marks. In many of the earliest manuscripts, there appears this Greek symbol η with a grave accent at the beginning of verse 36 to signal to the reader that the above statement is quoted.[113] In 1 Corinthians 14 we are caught in an intricate interplay between quotations from a missing letter from the Corinthians and Paul's solutions to the problems the letter had raised. The verse is clearly not repeating a law of Scripture and cannot be taken as a universal command for women to be silent in church because such an interpretation would flatly contradict what Paul had

---

[112] Ibid.

[113] Walter C. Kaiser, *Correcting Caricatures: The Biblical Teaching on Women*, Grand Rapids: Zondervan, 1981, p. 66.

just said three chapters earlier.[114] The same principle can be applied that the woman's silence may itself be significant.[115]

In 1Cor 14:33-35 Paul states that women should keep silence in church and be in subordination. The text reads as follows: -

> For God is not a God of confusion but of peace. As in all the churches of the saints, women should keep silence in the churches. For they are not permitted to speak, but should be subordinate, as even the law says. If there is anything they desire to know, let them ask their husbands at home. For it is shameful for a woman to speak in church.[116]

If indeed God is not a God of confusion as Paul observes, how can he appear to be in confusion himself by denying women to preach and demanding them to remain silent when at the same time he affirms that women should preach in chapter 11? It is clear from this context that Paul is saying women and men can pray and prophesy in public, as long as they follow proper behaviour and custom when doing so. Paul himself affirms that women were his co-workers in ministry (Romans 16). What then did Paul actually mean when he said that "women should remain silent in the churches," according to 1Cor 14:34 (NIV)?

The Need to Keep Silence

The text in context reveals that there was confusion in the Corinthian Church caused by speaking in tongues. Women were involved in this confusion. These women were those who especially claimed their Gnostic newfound rights. These women exercised their rights in a

---

[114] Kenneth Kantzer, "Proceed with Care," *Christianity Today*, 3.10.1986, p. 6.

[115] Joan E. Taylor, "The Woman ought to have Control over her Head because of the Angels (1 Corinthians 11:10)," in Douglas A. Campbell (ed), *Gospel and Gender: A Trinitarian Engagement with being Male and Female in Christ*, New York: T&T Clark, 2003, pp. 37-57, esp. pp. 49-57.

[116] 1 Cor 14:33-35.

manner that contradicted traditional roles of women in public. This attitude further contributed to the disorder in the church.[117] Another issue was the seating model in the church itself. Here, men and women sat separately from each other. Thus, verbal exchanges between husbands and wives, who sat separately on either side of the room, disrupted the worship service.[118] Furthermore, from the context of the letter to the Corinthians, Paul was attacking the claim of the members who were causing confusion due to speaking in tongues as in 1Cor 2, 3, and 12. Here, Paul stresses concern for others as an indispensable characteristic for a Christian.[119] Therefore, Paul's primary concern in Chapter 14 is to clarify a serious misunderstanding with regard to the *pneumatikoi* or "spiritual persons." In this context, Paul stresses the importance of doing everything in public worship for the building up of the congregation.[120]

Also, from the context of the whole letter, the command to keep silence is given to both men and women in some contexts. For example, in 1Cor 14:28 Paul wrote that "But if there is no one to interpret, let each of them keep silence in church and speak to himself and to God." In the second passage, 14:30, Paul also writes, "If a revelation is made to another sitting by, let the first keep silence." In both of these passages, the one told to "keep silence" is in the masculine gender. That means men are also required to keep silence so that order is maintained in the church.

---

[117] W. Larry Richards, "How Does a Woman Prophesy and Keep Silence at the Same Time? (1 Corinthians 11 and 14)," in Nancy Vyhmeister (ed), *Women in Ministry*, Berrien Springs: Andrews Uni, 1998, p. 323.

[118] Ibid.

[119] Ibid.

[120] Ibid.

The Meaning of Subordination

In 1Cor 14:34 Paul suggests that women "should be subordinate." Some have concluded from this text that Paul says women should be subordinate to all men in the church. Therefore, they are inferior to men and must always keep quiet before men. But this is not the meaning of the passage. In context, the subordination is to their husbands, not to men in general. The Greek word used here is *hupotasso*, "to subordinate," which has a variety of meanings. For example, submission is the correct thing for all Christians to do. Christians submit to God's law as in Romans 8:7: "For the mind that is set on the flesh is hostile to God; it does not submit to God's law, indeed, it cannot." Also, both men and women should submit to the governing powers mentioned in Romans 13:1-5: "Let every person be subject to the governing authorities. For there is no authority except from God, and those that exist have been instituted by God." (See also Titus 3:1; 1 Pet 2:13). In concluding his letter to the Corinthian church, Paul urges them to be subject to the household of Stephanas who is his associate in ministry (1Cor 16:16). Also, Paul admonishes Ephesian married couples, "Be subject to one another out of reverence for Christ" (Eph 5:21). This is a general injunction to mutual submission.[121] Even the prophetic spirit is to submit: "And the spirits of the prophets are subject to the prophets" (1Cor 14:32).

This kind of submission is related to the practice of self-discipline. Hence, submission in this context is something every Christian is expected to do for the benefit of others. Therefore, to say that Paul meant that women must submit to all men is contrary to the meaning of the text. Paul's aim was to discourage confusion in the church of God and bring order. The text does not say women must not preach the gospel.

---

[121] Ibid.

The Meaning of the Word "Prophesy"

In addition to the above interpretation, it is proper also to study the word "prophesy" in the same context in order to make sense and refute the idea that women must not preach in church. The word "prophecy" comes from the Hebrew word *'naba.'* It is from this word that the word *'nabi'* comes from. The word *'nabi'* means spokesman, speaker, or prophet.[122] For example, Moses objected to be *'nabi'* (God's spokesman) to the children of Israel (Ex 6:28-30). God declared that "Aaron, your brother, shall be your *'nabi'* (prophet)"(Ex 7:1,2). A *'nabi'* is a person authorized to speak for another.[123] The word *'nebia'* is a Hebrew word used for a prophetess; a woman who speaks for God.[124]

Thus, in 1Cor 14:37 the word used for prophet in Greek is translaterated as *'prophetes,'* meaning an inspired speaker.[125] But the speaking in 1Cor 14:34 is not inspired. Here women are commanded to keep silence and not to speak in church. The Greek word used here is *'laleo.'* It means to talk, utter words, or whisper in a general or informal way.[126] It may also mean to babble or make vocal utterances.[127]

The term used by Paul cannot mean preaching, because it was talking that was shameful. It was something the law forbade. If so, this could contradict what Paul had said before, that women could pray and preach (1Cor 11:5, 31). Moreover, both men and women would prophesy in the last days (Acts 2:18, 19). Paul was rebuking some

---

[122] Harries Laird et al, *Theological Wordbook of the Old Testament*, vol. 2, Chicago: Moody, 1980, p. 544.

[123] Ibid, p. 544.

[124] Ibid.

[125] Ibid.

[126] Ibid.

[127] William D. Mounce, *The Analytical Lexicon to the Greek New Testament*, Grand Rapids: Zondervan, 1993, p. 296.

women who were interrupting worship by whispering (or babbling), thus causing confusion in church.[128]

In fact, the restriction "Let your women keep silence in the churches" (v.34) targets only married women. The Greek word used for 'your women' is '*gune*.' Strong defines it as 'woman,' but specifically it is used for wives.[129] Thus the text can be read as "let your wives keep silence." Women must be silent in respect of their husbands who rule over them according to the law.

Many exegetes interpret 1 Corinthians 14:34-35 in conjunction with 1Timothy 2:8-15 to arrive at their view points about women's ministry in the church. But according to Ward Powers, Paul instructs that women are to remain silent in the churches. He believes that the word that Paul uses here, *sigao*, is defined in Newman's Dictionary as 'keep silent', 'be silent,' 'become silent', 'stop talking.' He contends that it is a quite different word from the word *hesuchia of* 1 Timothy 2:11-12, which means "quietness," not "silence." Taken at its absolute face value, this will mean that women must not utter any words of any kind in the assembly, and this instruction would thus rule out their participation not only in prayer but even in congregational singing.[130]

In respect to the above positions, Paul indeed allowed women to pray and prophesy in 1 Corinthians 11, but he did not give them permission to do so in public but only in private. Therefore, 1 Corinthians 14 gives an absolute prohibition against women speaking in public services.[131] He, however, fails to establish why he thinks Paul allowed women to

---

[128] Alexander R. Hay, *The Woman's Ministry in Church and Home*, Llandysul: Gomerian, 1962, p. 51.

[129] James Strong, *The Exhaustive Concordance of the Bible*, p. 21.

[130] Ward Powers, *The Ministry of Women in the Church: Which Way Forward?* Adelaide: SPCKA, 1996, pp. 58-59.

[131] F.W. Grosheide, *Commentary on the First Epistle to the Corinthians*, Grand Rapids: Zondervan, 1983, p. 342.

pray in private and not in public. Scholarship has established that it was not private praying that Paul allowed women to do.

There is no complete picture of what Paul says in this passage and why he says it. David Larson nevertheless suspects, as is evidenced by Paul's reference to the law, that to some extent Paul was appealing to Jewish custom.[132] He discredits this view by arguing that the term 'law' is never used in Paul's writings with reference to cultural customs. The law Paul had in mind is most likely the Old Testament principle of headship and subordination. Some commentators think that Paul was thinking of Genesis 3:16 that says, "Your husband ... shall rule over you" when he spoke of the law. Probably his strongest argument is that this notion is most unlikely because the New Testament never appeals to the 'curses' of the fall as a basis for Christian conduct or teaching.[133] Bacchiocchi, however, does not specify which law in the Old and New Testaments prohibits women to speak in the church.

The text under consideration in this study is located at the conclusion of a lengthy section of chapters 11 through 14 in which Paul deals with problem situations in the context of worship. Brauch observes that Paul had dealt with proper decorum of men and women while praying and prophesying in chapter 11:2-16; with irregularities at the Lord's Supper in chapter 11:17-34; with the nature, function, use, and abuse of spiritual gifts in chapters 12-14; and finally, with special consideration of the ecstatic phenomenon of speaking in tongues and prophecy in 14:1-25. In view of the foregoing, this shows that Paul is dealing with abuses and actions in worship which disrupt God's purposes and, therefore, need correction. He observes that within such a setting, our text seems clearly to belong to the category of 'corrective texts' whose purpose is focused toward a local situation. Paul's word that women

---

[132] David R. Larson, www.religioustolerance.org/hom_bibg.htm, [17.8.2015].

[133] Samuele Bacchiocchi, *Women in the Church: A Biblical Study on the Role of Women in the Church*, Berrien Springs: Biblical Perspectives, 1987, p. 169.

should remain silent in the churches would therefore seem, primarily, to have authoritative import for the particular situation in Corinth as well as in similar situations. He warns that one must be careful, therefore, not to jump to the conclusion immediately that Paul's injunction has implications for all women in all churches at all times.[134]

On women's participation in worship services, there is enough evidence from the writings of Paul and from practices in the early churches which show that women's vocal participation in worship and in other instructional or leadership roles was accepted and affirmed. Manfred Brauch points out that Paul himself acknowledges in this same letter the validity and appropriateness of women as full participants in public prayer and the proclamation of the gospel as noted in 1Cor 11:5, 13. His opinion is that what Paul finds invalid and unacceptable is that women engaged in this activity without a head covering, since that rejection of cultural religious custom creates a potential obstacle. He asserts that Paul affirms this view in 1Cor 11:16. In this context 'the churches of God' recognize no other practice than the appropriateness of a head covering for women who are praying and prophesying in church. He suggests that if Paul believed that women should be silent in the churches in a comprehensive, universal sense, he would not have spent so much time in chapter 11 instructing women what to do with their heads. He would have simply forbidden their practice of praying and prophesying in the assembled congregations.[135]

In light of evidence in Scripture from Acts 2:21 and Joel 2 women in the early churches were moved by the Spirit to engage in ministries of the Word side by side with men. It is difficult, if not impossible, to understand Paul's injunction as a categorical imperative intended for all churches in all places at all times. He, therefore, concludes that the

---

[134] Manfred Brauch, *Hard Sayings of Paul,* Toronto: Hodder and Stoughton, 1990, pp. 167-168.

[135] Ibid, pp. 167-168.

injunction must be understood within its own context as addressing a problem in Corinth which needed correcting. He suggests that the particular issue in this case consisted of such elements as disorder, lack of regularity, and confusion in public worship. He suggests that this situation was apparently caused by the inappropriate expression of both the gift of prophecy and of speaking in tongues as in 14:26–31. The suggestion he gives is that the admonition to women's silence is in some way related to women's participation in the inappropriate use of these gifts.[136] The view Brauch brings forth is significant. He suggests that if, as seems likely, women were prominent in the group of prophets judged to be disorderly, Paul may, in 14:34, be addressing them specifically with regard to this matter of submission to other prophets for the sake of order and peace which he calls for in 14:33, 34. This, he notes, may suggest that the problem of disorderly participation in prophetic proclamation and tongues was particularly prominent among women believers in Corinth, and that it is with respect to this context that Paul's admonitions must be understood.[137]

The intent of Paul's command is to confront situations in which wives publicly contradicted what their husbands said or thought or embarrassed them by an interchange of conversation. Hilary Mijoga suggests that wives debated with their husbands in a public forum like this one. This amazed husbands as well as the church because it was a strange practice. With the kind of behaviour that wives displayed in this chapter, it is possible that they may thus have rejected the authority of their husbands, an authority which was firmly fixed in the practice of their religion. They were no longer subordinate to their husbands.[138]

---

[136] Ibid, p. 170.

[137] Ibid, p. 171.

[138] Hilary B.P. Mijoga, "Gender Differentiation in the Bible: Created and Recognized," in Jonathan S. Nkhoma, *Significance of the Dead Sea Scrolls and*

Hilary Mijoga suggests that this is what prompted Paul to remind the church that "women are not allowed (by the Jewish and Greek cultures) to speak as the law says for it is disgraceful (in the Greek and Jewish cultures) for a woman to speak in the church."[139] He concludes that the sensible assumption is that Paul made such an injunction on wives to preserve order and decorum in the worship service which was the subject under discussion here.[140]

The context of this passage seems to favour the view that the tongues experience was leading to the understanding that women did it out of line with the traditional roles of women in public. Ronald Pierce assumes that if the synagogue model was followed where men and women were separated during public services, then any verbal exchanges between husbands on one side of the room and wives on the other obviously would have been disrupting. This assumption of a synagogue model is not supported. This proposal appears to be unsatisfactory. Although the Corinthian church started in a synagogue (Acts 18:4), it now met in homes as in Acts 18:7, which would hardly afford the space for such gender segregation. House churches were undoubtedly less formal but apparently included a teaching element that would probably follow many practices familiar from similarly sized learning gatherings in the culture.[141] In these circumstances women or wives would still assert their Gnostic views because questions were common in Jewish settings in particular and were a regular part of ancient Mediterranean lecture settings in general.

Other Essays. Biblical and Early Christianity Studies from Malawi, Mzuzu: Mzuni Press, 2013, p. 192.

[139] Ibid, p. 192.

[140] Ibid.

[141] Ronald W. Pierce et al (eds), *Discovering Biblical Equality: Complementarily without Hierarchy*, Leicester: InterVarsity, 2004, pp. 161-162, 167-168.

This discussion reveals that as the church was growing in membership in Corinth, many cultural and traditional problems crept into it because those who were converted to the church brought into it their former practices and beliefs. These were dealt with according to time and place. As women were exposed to early forms of Gnosticism as taught by false teachers they came in with great zeal and started asking questions or asserting their newfound teaching in the church during worship time in public. Paul made an injunction against this practice, for it was shameful for a woman to speak during worship. Though these were Christian gatherings, change from old ways of worship to more convenient and inclusive practices had to be done cautiously, slowly, and carefully. Therefore, the injunction that Paul made was just in time to protect God's church and does not apply to all times. The prohibition against women's speaking in church cannot be absolute, for Paul had just given instructions in chapter 11 for the veiling of women so that they may pray and prophesy in public worship.[142]

Interpretations of 1 Timothy 2:8-15

The contemporary debate over the role of women in the church has boggled the minds of Biblical scholars. Paul writes this first letter to his disciple and co-worker, Timothy, to remind him "how people ought to conduct themselves in God's household " (1 Timothy 3:15).

To have an understanding of 1Tim 2, there is need to know the religious power of women in the Greco-Roman World.[143] Kroeger asserts that women assumed roles as the prime movers in religion, those who played an initiatory and introductory role.[144] Young maidens were said

---

[142] Robert H. Gundry, *A Survey of the New Testament,* Grand Rapids: Zondervan, 1981, p. 268.

[143] Catherine Kroeger, "The Apostle Paul and the Greco-Roman World Cults of Women": 30-1-pp. 025-038-JETS.pdf (Paul and the Cults of Women), March 1987, pp. 25-38, esp. p. 31.

[144] Ibid, p. 31.

to have brought Demeter into the city of Eleusis, and women are credited with having introduced the cult of Dionysos into Italy and Greece. The mother of Aeschines was responsible for the entry of the Sabazios Cult into Athens, while Roman matrons played a major role in gaining a place for Cybele in the Roman pantheon.[145] The religious influence of women in Asia Minor was also enormous.[146] Women were not usually allowed to consult oracles, yet only they could deliver them at the famed shrines in Dodona and Delphi. This was a sign of superiority for women.[147] The mediatorial role of women was important throughout the history of Greek religion.[148] This gave women a sort of religious one-up-manship that carried into Gnosticism, where a female figure was often the messenger of divine revelation.[149] The writer of the Pastorals may have had this in mind when he stated that Paul had been sent to the Gentiles as herald and teacher of the truth that there is one God and one mediator (1Tim 2:4-7). Immediately after this statement he gives separate directives for the behaviour of Gentile men and women (1Tim 2:8-11). There is a certain amount of evidence in the context that this prohibition in 1Tim 2:12 is directed against women who claimed a feminine spirituality and power of creation superior to that of males.[150]

Paul sends this reminder because the church at Ephesus where Timothy was left to continue the work of ministry was beset with false teachings.[151] It is, therefore, correct to infer that 1 Timothy was written,

---

[145] Ibid, p. 32.

[146] Ibid, p. 31.

[147] Ibid.

[148] Ibid.

[149] Ibid, p. 32.

[150] Ibid, p. 32.

[151] Nancy Jean Vyhmeister (ed), *Women in Ministry: Proper Church Behaviour in 1 Timothy 2:8-15*, Berrien Springs: Andrews, 1998, p. 336.

as elucidated by chapter 1:1-7, to counter the sinister influence of certain false teachers upon the church at Ephesus. Upon reading 1 Timothy, one becomes immediately aware that the integrity of the Christian faith is at stake.[152] Chapter 1 shows clearly that there are some in the church at Ephesus who teach false doctrines and are preoccupied with myths and other speculative ideas which militate against sound and sincere faith. For this reason, some wandered into vain debates, seeking to be teachers without understanding and discernment. The result of such teachings was that other members wandered away into vain discussion. Concerned over the disruptive influence of these false teachings in the life of the church, Paul wrote to Timothy, his delegated representative, giving him instructions on how to order and direct the life of a Christian congregation. The false doctrine that went around at Ephesus found fertile ground in vulnerable women because they were generally less literate, therefore, less informed, and vulnerable to false teachings.[153]

It is probable that these false teachers included mild Gnosticism because Paul wrote this letter to Timothy when Gnosticism was just beginning to establish itself. However, in the first century, when Paul wrote this letter to Timothy, Gnosticism was still an aggregate of loosely related religious ideas rather than a highly organized system of doctrine.[154] Gundry states that 1 Timothy and other pastoral letters attack a type of Gnosticism that arose only after Paul's lifetime though during this time Gnosticism was not fully grown. He argues that the asceticism criticized in 1 Timothy 4:3, which forbids marriage and advocates

---

[152] Manfred Brauch, *Hard Sayings of Paul,* Toronto: Hodder and Stoughton, 1990, p. 255.

[153] Samuele Bacchiocchi, *Women in the Church: A Biblical Study on the Role of Women in the Church,* Berrien Springs: Biblical Perspectives, 1987, p. 145.

[154] Robert H. Gundry, *A Survey of the New Testament,* Grand Rapids: Zondervan, 1981, p. 37.

abstaining from foods, sounds somewhat like later Gnosticism.[155] While Gundry may be correct in his assumption that Gnosticism was one of the errors which crept into the church of Ephesus, it is important to note as well that it was not the main false teaching that false teachers were teaching vulnerable women since the system was not full-blown.

Given women's lack of training in the Scriptures, the heresy spreading in the Ephesian churches through ignorant teachers, and false teachers' exploitation of these women's lack of knowledge to spread their errors, perhaps Paul's prohibition here makes good sense. Keener suggests that Paul's short-range solution is to forbid these women to teach, but his long-range solution is to 'let them learn' because the situation might be different after the women have been instructed.[156] Guthrie also agrees with the view that the prohibition may have been due to the greater speed with which contemporary women were falling under the influence of impostors.[157]

In 1 Timothy 2:11, 12 women are given the chance to learn Scripture. They had a strong thirst for knowledge to the extent that they entertained false teachers. The tone of the passage suggests that the Christian church, unlike the Jewish faith, gave women the right to learn together with the male members of the congregation. Therefore, according to Paul, the solution to the inroads that the false teachers were making among the women was not to forbid them to listen to the false teachers and then keep them in ignorance, but rather to develop their knowledge of the truth through teachers well trained. In order for

---

[155] Ibid, p. 306.

[156] Craig S. Keener, *The IVP Bible Background Commentary, New Testament*, Downers Grove: InterVarsity Press, 1993, p. 611.

[157] Donald Guthrie, *The Pastoral Epistles*, Leicester: InterVarsity, Eerdmans, 1984, p. 76.

that learning to be effective, Paul recommended that women should learn in silence.[158]

In 1Tim 2:11, 12 the issue of women's submission is presented differently from what one might expect because the context presents it as a learning situation. The context does not suggest that women are prohibited to teach their husbands as some suggest. Paul refers to a family setting and not a church setting. Frank Chirwa suggests that this means that Paul is prohibiting women from teaching their husbands at home, not at church.[159] This notion distorts the whole meaning of the passage. The weakness of this position is that the context of the passage is not taken into consideration. Again, the passage talks about submission to men and not to husbands. These men, according to the context, should be teachers because many teachers were men during the time. This suggests that women were teaching but were not conversant with what was sound doctrine to be taught. Therefore, they were forbidden to teach to avoid misleading the church. The passage does not suggest a husband-wife relationship but a teacher-student relationship. The injunction does not come in because of the common notion that women must be submissive, per se, to men. It is common knowledge that for a student to learn much from a teacher, he/she must learn in submission to the teacher who knows much more than the student. Stubborn students do not learn much and disturb other students as well. The submission spoken of here is to be given to their teachers. These are married women who are under the instruction of male teachers. At the same time Paul does not allow them to teach because they are novices. Sometimes students teach one another very well if they are not under misleading influences. In our passage, women

---

[158] Ibid, p. 77.

[159] Frank Chirwa, "Church Conflict: Its Relationship to Women's Participation in Ministry in the Seventh-day Adventist Churches in Malawi," MA, Solusi University, 2005, p. 48.

were under the influence of false teachers, probably Gnostic teachers, and, therefore, to let them teach one another would lead to controversy and confusion (1Tim 1:3-11). This is why Paul says "I do not allow a woman to teach." The principle that Paul applies here can as well be applied in our time if factors that prompted Paul to speak the way he did would arise because peace must reign in a learning environment. The submission enjoined on women is a submission of women to the elders in the church who are guardians of the truth and of ordered worship. The prohibition against their teaching is occasioned by their involvement in false teachings. The prohibition against 'authority over a man' must be understood within the context of women's rejection of authority of elders in Ephesus whose authoritative teaching was undermined by their heretical views.[160]

If one needs further understanding of the assumed statement against women by the apostle Paul, the religious background needs to be analyzed before making conclusions by silencing women in church in general terms. The socio-religious setting in Ephesus was characterized by pagan worship. Most prominent was the cult of the mother goddess Artemis or Diana. It was later assimilated into Judaism and finally into Gnosticism.[161]

This popularity of Artemis is attested by Luke in Acts 19:23-41. Here, Luke records the "stir" of the silversmiths and the populace of Ephesus in support of Artemis, who is affirmed as the one "whom all Asia and the world worship." Artemis was called a virgin, not necessarily that she was indeed a virgin, but rather because she had not submitted to a husband. The belief was, "No bonds tied Artemis to any male she would

---

[160] Manfred Brauch, *Hard Sayings of Paul,* Toronto: Hodder and Stoughton, 1990, pp. 168.

[161] Carolyn Osiek, "The Feminist and the Bible: Hermeneutical Alternatives" in Adela Y. Collins (ed), *Feminist Perspectives on Biblical Scholarship: Society of Biblical Literature*, Chico: Scholars, 1985, pp. 65-92.

have to acknowledge as master."[162] Thus, her worship required a multitude of priests and priestesses and other attendants. Each year a month was dedicated to Artemis, in which there were cultic rituals including athletic, dramatic, and musical contests. Women were especially attracted to her worship since she was perceived as "chaste, beautiful, and intelligent." She was believed to meet the needs of the female worshippers.[163]

In addition, the ultimate cult power of Artemis worship was assumed by a high priestess. The *Artemision* and its cult made Ephesus "the bastion and bulwark of women's rights."[164] It was in the context of such a religious setting that tales and fables were highly entertained. This is because many of the most popular Greek myths were placed in Asia Minor and these were told and retold. This is why Ephesus figures prominently in ancient novels, such as Xenophon's *Ephesian Tale* (4th century B.C.).[165] Horace (65 B.C.) noted that old women who retold myths and stories were remarkably able to shape their material according to their own situation.[166] While these stories were mostly told for entertainment, the stories also contained theological ingredients which shaped religious opinion.[167]

---

[162] Ibid.

[163] Ibid.

[164] Markus Barth, "Ephesians," *Anchor Bible*, Garden City: Doubleday, 1974, 2; 661; this conclusion not withstanding claims to the contrary made by S.M. Baugh, "A Foreign World: Ephesus in the First Century," in Andreas J. Köstenberger, Thomas R. Schreiner, and H. Scott Baldwin (eds), *Women in the Church: A Fresh Analysis of 1 Timothy 2:9-15*, Grand Rapids: Baker, 1995, pp. 13-63.

[165] Ibid.

[166] Horace Satires 2. 6. 77-78 Cited in Vyhmeister, "Proper Church Behavior in 1 Timothy 2: 8-15, " p. 338.

[167] *Cicero on the Nature of the Gods* 3. 5. 12-13. Cited in Vyhmeister, p. 338

Consequently, on the western coast of Asia Minor, there was a tradition of dominant women. These were women warriors who dominated the males.[168] These legends did not just circulate as stories but were perceived as actual history.[169] For example, Artemisia of Halicarnassus is said to have fought alongside Xerxes – as commander of five ships and also as Xerxes' advisor. This battle was fought at Salamis, the Greeks won, in spite of Artemisia's help to Xerxes.

Also, in the tradition of Hercules and Omphale, Hercules was forced to be subject to the Lydian queen and to ply the shuttle and the ferry. His acceptance of servitude to a woman was believed to bring about purification.[170] This background to Paul's statement on women may also have been the context of an early-second century AD Hymn to Isis. Isis was often identified with Artemis. As a goddess identified with Isis, Artemis was believed to vest women with power equal to that of men.[171] It was therefore in this context that Paul talked about the need of some women being silent and subject to men, when he wrote his epistle to Timothy. Because of this context I argue that Paul never told women not to preach the gospel in church. He was rebuking and denouncing the attitude of some women and that this should not be perpetuated in the church of God.

The challenge of women in church and their relationship to their husbands can also be analyzed in the context that there were Gnostic ideas that flourished during the 1st century, which caused Paul to admonish Timothy (1Tim 6:2) to avoid the godless chatter and contradictions

---

[168] *Diodorus of Sicily* 3. 52. 4-54. 7. Cited in Vyhmeister, p. 33.

[169] *Strabo Geography* 11. 5. 3. Cited in Vyhmeister, p. 338.

[170] Richard Clark Kroeger and Catherine Clark Kroeger, *I Suffer Not a Woman*, Grand Rapids: Baker, 1992, pp. 194-195.

[171] "Invocation of Isis," papyrus 1380, *Oxyrhynchus Papyri*, London: Egypt Exploration Fund, 1915, 11: 214-216. Cited in Vyhmeister, p. 339.

of what is falsely called knowledge (*gnosis*). For example, Gnostic statements were designed to exalt Eve's part in creation. In one of these statements, Adam addresses Eve saying, "You are the one who has given life."[172] There were also some teachings taught from the Gospel of the Egyptians. This gospel claims that Jesus said, "I came to destroy the works of the female." Jesus then points out that death will prevail as long as women bear children. To this declaration Salome responds by saying, "Then I have done well in bearing no children."[173]

Also, according to the Gospel of Thomas (ca. AD 140), it is claimed that Peter wanted to send Mary away "because women are not worthy of life." But Jesus offered to make her into a male, "because every woman who will make herself male shall enter into the kingdom of heaven."[174] Therefore, femaleness was seen as a defect and that salvation came through masculinity, or better still through the elimination of all sexuality.[175] The Gnostic teachings were so intriguing to the extent that *Epiphanius* (ca. 315-403) tells of a Gnostic group which was hated by the Ephesus church and which disturbed *Pergamum* (Rev 2:6, 15), whom he calls successors to the *Nicolaitans*. It was these people who rejected marriage. They were also opposed to childbearing. Furthermore, they practiced what is called *coitus interruptus* and went as far as to abort the foetus of a pregnant woman.[176]

The aim of the apostle Paul then is to emphasize that women in the Ephesus congregations should learn that the excesses of *Artemis* worship, along with its ascetic or sensual practices, were inappropriate for Christian women. Also, those from the Jewish background needed

---

[172] *Hypostasis of the Archons* 2. 4. 89. 14-17. Cited in Vyhmeister, p. 339.

[173] *Clement of Alexandria Miscellanies* 3. 45. Cited in Vyhmeister, p. 339.

[174] *Gospel of Thomas* 114, cited in Vyhmeister, p. 339.

[175] *Dialogue of the Savior* 90-95; *Gospel of Thomas* 27. Cited in Vyhmeister, p. 339.

[176] Epiphanius Panarion 26. 3-5. Cited in Vyhmeister, p. 340.

the encouragement "to study, learn, and serve in the Christian community."[177] It is then to such a context that the apostle Paul wrote about women in the manner he did. He never desired women who were his esteemed co-workers in the gospel work not to preach the gospel in church or anywhere else.

In his epistle to Timothy Paul therefore begins his pastoral advice with general instructions and exhortations for public prayer, especially for the elders or those in authority in the church. In verse 8 he says that men are to lift up their hands, without anger or quarrelling. He said this in the context of the tension that was within the Ephesus church.[178] This exhortation was delivered both for men as well as women. It was gender inclusive. This is very evident in the context of the following verses 9 and 10 on the attitude of both men and women in prayer:

> I desire then that in every place the men should pray, lifting holy hands without anger or quarrelling; also, that women should adorn themselves modestly and sensibly in seemly apparel, not with braided hair or gold or pearls or costly attire but by good deeds, as befits women who profess religion (vv. 9-10 RSV).

In this passage, Paul gives instructions to both men and women when engaged in prayer or worship. Initially, he addresses gender inclusiveness, when church members are engaged in public prayer and worship. Hence, the attitude of men and the way women are adorned both play a vital part in that engagement. What is therefore said for men is also said for women when engaged in public worship or prayer. He is not refusing the privilege of women to engage in preaching.

But what is problematic for most Christians is what Paul means when he concludes that women must learn *in silence* in verse 11 of this chapter. This verse says, "Let a woman learn in silence with all

---

[177] Nancy Vyhmeister (ed), *Women in Ministry*, Berrien Springs: Andrews, 1998; Mijoga, p. 340.

[178] Ibid, p. 341.

submissiveness" (RSV). It is, however, clear from this passage that Paul allows Jewish women to learn. But it is the manner or attitude in learning that is here brought into question. That is, women should learn in silence. It was in the same attitude that women had the privilege to learn in silence before Jesus like Mary and other women (Lk 8:1-3; 10:39). Paul approves the same attitude in learning for women in this passage.

1 Timothy 2:8-12 states that men should pray everywhere. Sin could hinder their prayers. Following this is a transition phrase that says, "in like manner also ... women." This entails that what has been said for men is also true for women in praying. Both men and women pray everywhere, whether in church or out of church (1Cor 11:5; Eph 6:18, 19; Col 4:2-4 and 1 Thess 5:17). However, before her husband, the woman should learn in quietness and in all subjection.

The Greek word for silence used in this passage is '*hesuchia*.' Used as a noun, it means stillness, a peaceable and quiet environment.[179] It is not the same word as used in 1Cor 14:28, 30, 34 which is '*sigawo*', to keep silence, a hush situation.[180] This refers to the Greek word rendered '*siope*' meaning 'involuntary silence.'[181] The latter is an ordered or commanded situation hence 'involuntary silence.' The reference is in a family setting, not in church as said in 1Cor 14:34-35. She should not seek or desire to teach her husband, nor be domineering or bossy. Clearly, the text does not say that the woman should not preach in the church.[182]

---

[179] Ibid, p. 35.

[180] Ibid, p. 65.

[181] Ibid.

[182] Alexander R. Hay, *The Woman's Ministry in the Church and Home*, Llandysul: Gomerian Press, 1962, p. 57.

Paul's inclusive missionary approach is more appreciated when it is viewed juxtaposed between the religious and socio-cultural chasms that negatively impacted upon Jews, Gentiles, women and slaves. These must be engaged together in the eschatological vision of Paul's inclusive ministry and his view on God's inclusive ministry. Hence, in such a context, Paul is propelled by his belief that God does not segregate gender, race, and ethnicity when this relates to salvation of all humankind and gospel ministry (Gal 3:28; Mt 28:18-20). Following after Paul, Peter is also able to affirm, "I now realize how true it is that God does not show favouritism but accepts men from every nation who fear Him and do what is right ... So, if God gave them the same gift as He gave us ... who was I to think that I could oppose God (Acts 10:34, 35; 11:17 NIV).

Paul was actually preparing women to be good teachers once they learned the Scriptures. This does not mean Paul forbade women in all Christendom to teach at all times. Paul lays enough emphasis on the principle of reverence and decorum during worship as in 1Cor 14:33–34. Men and women who were instructed understood Paul better than we do today because they understood the situation in which they were. The injunctions that Paul gave were well received for the passage as the entire epistle does not give us mixed reactions by women or men against them. This passage teaches that peace and tranquillity should prevail where God is worshipped or where the study of Scripture is done. It is common knowledge and practice that in a discussion or debate where substantive ideas are contributed those who have no knowledge about the subject should keep silent and learn in silence and submission, perhaps questions can be asked.

This study has established that Paul was dealing with particular situations that arose in the Ephesian and Corinthian churches. In these particular scenarios, Paul wanted to bring to an end the work of false teachers in Ephesus, bring harmony among husbands and wives at Corinth, and bring order to worship services in both churches. It has been established that Paul himself involved women in his ministries. I submit that these admonitions can be understood to be in harmony with the clear affirmations of the presence of women as disciples, teachers, prophets, deacons, (one) apostle, along with the possibility of women elders. In this manner, the Pauline texts considered can be seen as supportive of the great vision in Gal 3:28 where 'in Christ ... there is no longer male and female for all of you are one in Christ Jesus.'[183]

---

[183] Kenneth E. Bailey, "Women in the New Testament: A Middle Eastern Cultural View," in *Theology Matters: A Publication of Presbyterians for Faith, Family and Ministry*, vol. 6, no 1, Jan/Feb 2000, pp. 1-10, esp. p. 10.

Chapter 5

Toward a Theology of Gender in CCAP Zambia

This chapter attempts a reconstruction of Gender Theology for CCAP Zambia in light of the findings of the current study as revealed in the previous chapters.

The concern in this study was to find out factors that make members have divergent positions on ordination and ministry of women and why some Pauline texts are used to oppress women in the church, leading some to accusing Paul of having hated women, and of supporting the oppression of women. The research revealed that problems and challenges still exist perpetuated against women.

In chapter two, the research revealed religious and cultural reasons. Most Pauline writings are literalistically interpreted to discourage women from taking part in ordained ministry, and to deprive them of higher leadership positions. This is the case in CCAP Zambia although the Synod allows women's ordination. Although some women ministry can be noticed, the few female ministers who are ordained still face challenges. There is no inclusiveness. Women themselves are not supporting each other to push this agenda forward. Most members are unaware of the position of CCAP Zambia on women. Those interested often lack necessary academic qualifications and some lack confidence. Those already in ministry are accused of not being good models, being perceived as having bad temperaments and lacking self-control. This study also revealed that Holy Ministry is not attractive in terms of good conditions of service. In view of this, the study has shown some challenges. On one hand, people's mindset has not changed concerning women. It is considered scandalous for the female ministers to become pregnant. It is also difficult for a single woman minister to find marriage or to visit Christians with the Session Clerk if he is male. Transportation is a challenge for women if they are posted into remote areas. On the other hand, married ministers' postings and transfers become a challenge and they fail to maintain their family bonds. However, their performance is good. The study has also shown the continuous conflict between the biblical message of female male equality and some elements of the cultures of today.

In chapter four, this study revealed literal biblical interpretations that support the *status quo*. The Pauline texts such as 1Cor 11:2-11; 1Cor 14:34-35 and 1Tim 2:8-15 are oppressively interpreted against women. The study has shown continuous conflict in 1Cor 11:2-11 with Paul being accused of perpetuating a theology of headship or subordinationism against women. But this study has shown that Paul gave women authority over their own heads (1Cor 11:10) whether to cover the head or not. Paul told them exactly the opposite because the Greek word *exousia* in 1Cor 11:10, and elsewhere in the New Testament means authority and power (Matt 7:29; Matt 9:6; Matt 10:1; Matt 11:13 and John 1:12). This shows that women were not compelled to put on headgear nor was it a sign of submission. It was a choice to show the modesty of a woman.[1] This study has shown that CCAP Zambia can find for this alternative interpretation a space in their theology. This is in line with Paul's Theology of inclusiveness and liberation of women in the Church as reflected in Gal 3:28.

This study has shown that Paul in 1Cor 14:34-35 is again often misinterpreted with regard to the theology of silence that requires women not to speak in church. This study, however, has shown that Paul could not contradict himself since he had already given instructions in Chapter 11 for the veiling of women so that they may pray and

---

[1] See Rachel NyaGondwe Fiedler et al, *African Feminist Hermeneutics: An Evangelical Reflection*, Mzuzu: Mzuni Press, p. 114. Also, Joan E. Taylor, "The Woman ought to have Control over her Head because of the Angels" (1 Corinthians 11:10), in Douglas A. Campbell (ed), *Gospel and Gender: A Trinitarian Engagement with being Male and Female in Christ,* New York: T&T Clark, 2003, pp. 37-57, esp. pp. 49-57.

prophesy in public worship.² The study has established that Paul does not contradict himself as he preached liberation of women. This study argues that the same spirit needs to be seen in CCAP Zambia. The study has shown that Paul's statements need to be studied in light of the context of the phenomena and practices of ancient women.

The research has also revealed that there is incorrect understanding of the Greco-Roman world cults surrounding the religious activities of women. Pauline mandates must be examined both in the light of the NT writings and against a background of contemporary attitudes and practice.³

The study has established that a Historical-Critical reading of these texts, especially Gal 3:28, reveals that an alternative Pauline Gender Theology in CCAP Zambia is possible. This research has established that this text is liberative. Paul hopes for liberation from each of the three categories. Gal 3:28 supports an egalitarianism of function in the church. It offers women a revolution and Paul provides a breakthrough.⁴ On one hand, this study has shown that some men have started accepting women in ordained ministry. It is clearly Paul's most radical statement about gender identity and roles and the Magna Charta of women capable of being responsive to the existing conditions in church

---

[2] Robert H. Gundry, *A Survey of the New Testament,* Grand Rapids: Zondervan, 1981, p. 37.

[3] Catherine Kroeger, "The Apostle Paul and the Greco-Roman World Cults of Women" (Paul and the Cults of Women), March 1987, pp. 25-38.

[4] See Int. Rev Getrude N. Banda, Chasefu CCAP Congregation, Lundazi, 24.5.2015; Jeremy Barrier, in Musa Dube, *Postcolonial Feminist Interpretation of the Bible,* St. Louis: Chalice 2008, pp. 336-362; Wayne Grudem, *Systematic Theology: An Introduction to Biblical Doctrine*, Leicester: InterVarsity, 1994, pp. 458-459; Robert Jewett, "The Sexual Liberation of the Apostle Paul," *Journal of American Academy of Religion*, no. 47, 1979, pp. 53-87.

and society.⁵ On the other hand, this study has also shown that Gal 3:28 is not only a comfort to women as it removes discriminations since Paul is speaking of equal privileges between men and women, but also shows that Paul believed that gender distinctions cease in Christ.⁶ This study has established that Gal 3:28 is not only abolitionist and therefore political but is also liberational text.⁷ This study has further revealed that Gal 3:28 is the necessary theological starting place for any discussion on the role of women in the Church. This research has revealed three important issues underpinning Paul's reasoning as the basis of his Theology: Liberation, Responsiveness and Inclusiveness.

This research argues for an alternative understanding of these texts to achieve equal respect for all, equal opportunities for all and equal roles for all. The people in the church should be on the same level. That is the vision of Pauline Theology for CCAP Zambia. In CCAP Zambia, the church should be responsive, liberative and inclusive in order to reconstruct a

---

⁵ See Int. Rev Susan Nyirenda Tembo, Luanshya CCAP Congregation, Luanshya, 24.5.2015; Judith M. Gundry-Volf, "Beyond Difference? Paul's Vision of a New Humanity in Galatians 3:28," in Douglas A. Campbell(ed), *Gospel and Gender: A Trinitarian Engagement with being Male and Female in Christ,* New York: T&T Clark, 2003, pp. 8-36, esp. 34-36; Rachel NyaGondwe Fiedler et al, *African Feminist Hermeneutics: An Evangelical Reflection*, Mzuzu: Mzuni Press, p. 115

⁶ See Rev Naomi Daka, Mazabuka CCAP Congregation, Mazabuka, Southern Province, 18.5.2015; These were the 9 out of the 27 Synod leaders interviewed; Hilary Mijoga, "Gender Differentiation in the Bible: Created," in Jonathan S. Nkhoma, *Significance of the Dead Sea Scrolls and Other Essays*, Mzuzu: Mzuni Press, 2013, pp. 176-198, esp. pp. 191-198; Bernadette J. Brooten, "Early Christian Women and Their Cultural Context: Issues of Method in Historical Reconstruction," in Adela Y. Collins (ed), *Feminist Perspectives on Biblical Scholarship*: Society of Biblical Literature, Chico: Scholars, 1985 pp. 65-92 [86].

⁷ Douglas A. Campbell, "The Logic of Eschatology; The Implication of Paul's Gospel for Gender as Suggested by Galatians 3:28a in Context," in Douglas A. Campbell(ed), *Gospel and Gender: A Trinitarian Engagement with being Male and Female in Christ*, pp. 58-81, New York: T&T Clark, 2003, esp. pp. 69.

new humanity where ethnicity, power and gender are no longer sources of division.

If women are to be liberated in CCAP Zambia, this is the Theology to adopt. This will point to an ideal Church where there are no divisions, where texts are read liberatively and where the vision of Paul regarding gender equality is achieved. This theology offers that basis.

The objective of the study, to offer to CCAP Zambia members an understanding of gender equality based on Paul's theology in the passages literalistically seen to bar women from church participation on an equal basis with men in light of Galatians 3:28, was achieved. This book will provide, chiefly for the members of the CCAP, sister churches, scholars and others interested in Pauline gender theology, an alternative understanding of Paul's hard sayings using a Historical-Critical approach. To this long felt need this study has contributed. This can solve the problem that we started with in CCAP Zambia.

Bibliography

Unpublished

Banda, Oswald Jimmy, "The Role of Women in the Anglican Diocese of Northern Malawi," MA, Mzuzu University, 2013.

Chilenje, Victor, "A History of the Church of Central Africa Presbyterian (CCAP) in Zambia 1880s-1998," BTh, Justo Mwale Theological College, 1998.

Chilenje, Victor, "The Origin and Development of Church of Central Africa Presbyterian in Zambia 1882-2004," DTh, University of Stellenbosch, 2007.

Chirwa, Frank, "A Critical Examination of the Changing Role of Women in the Seventh-day Adventist Church in Malawi: A Historical, Theological, and Social-Cultural Analysis," PhD, Mzuzu University, 2014.

Chirwa, Frank, "Church Conflict: Its Relationship to Women's Participation in Ministry in the Seventh-day Adventist Churches in Malawi," MA, Solusi University, 2005.

Fiedler, Rachel NyaGondwe, "The Circle of Concerned African Women Theologians (1989-2007): History and Theology," PhD, University of the Free State, 2010.

Int. Rev C.T. Soko, Synod Executive Member, Matero CCAP Congregation, Lusaka, 9.7.2015.

Int. Rev David Chiboboka, CTC Principal and former General Secretary CCAP Zambia, Lundazi, 15.5.2015; 30.7.2015.

Int. Rev Dr V. Chilenje, Synod Moderator, Justo Mwale University, Lusaka, 17.8.2015; 10.7.2015.

Int. Rev Getrude N. Banda, Chasefu CCAP Congregation, Lundazi, 24.5.2015.

Int. Rev Kondwani Nkhoma, Kalulushi CCAP Congregation, Kitwe, 24.5.2015.

Int. Rev L.M. Nyirenda, Retired Synod Moderator, Mphamba CCAP Congregation, Lundazi, 10.6.2015.

Int. Rev M.R. Kabandama, General Secretary, Synod Offices, Lusaka, 17.7.2015/ 18.5.2015/ 13.8.2015.

Int. Rev Naomi Daka, Mazabuka CCAP Congregation, Mazabuka, Southern Province, 18.5.2015.

Int. Rev S.M. Mithi, First Synod Moderator CCAPZ, Chipata CCAP Congregation, 22.5.2015.

Int. Rev Susan Nyirenda Tembo, Luanshya CCAP Congregation, Luanshya, 24.5.2015.

Int. Rev T.T. Chipeta, Chitala CCAP Congregation, Lundazi, 21.5.2015.

Int. Susan Tembo Nyirenda, Luanshya CCAP Congregation, Luanshya, 24.5.-2015.

Int. Thandiwe Chipeta, Chitala CCAP Congregation, Lundazi, 21.5.2015.

Minutes 29/92 of the CCAP Livingstonia Synod of 18-23 August, 1992.

Minutes of Chasefu Presbytery of the Church of Central Africa Presbyterian Synod of Livingstonia, 17th -21st June 1981 CCAPLA.

Minutes of General Administration Committee of 3-7 April 1984.

Minutes of the 10th CCAP Zambia Synod held at Lundazi Boma from 20th to 25th August, 2002.

Minutes of the 11th Synod meeting held at Chipata Teachers Training College from 24th to 29th August, 2004.

Minutes of the General Administration Committee of 1-5 April 1992.

Minutes of the General Administration Committee of 16-20 April 1985.

Mwangombo, Chance, "The Life and Work of the Rev Wedson Paul Chibambo and Lucy Chibambo of the CCAP Synod of Livingstonia," BTh, University of Livingstonia, 2013.

Published

Arndt, William F., Wilbur F. Gingrich, *A Greek - English Lexicon of the New Testament and other Early Christian Literature*, Fourth Revised and augmented edition, Chicago: The University of Chicago Press, 1952.

Bacchiocchi, Samuele, *Women in the Church: A Biblical Study on the Role of Women in the Church*, Berrien Springs: Biblical Perspectives, 1987.

Bailey, Kenneth E., "Women in the New Testament: A Middle Eastern Cultural View," in *Theology Matters: A Publication of Presbyterians for Faith, Family and Ministry*, vol. 6, no 1, Jan/Feb 2000, pp. 1-10.

Banda, Rachel NyaGondwe [Fiedler], *Women of Bible and Culture*, Zomba: Kachere, 2005.

Barrett, C.K., *First Epistle to the Corinthians,* 2nd ed, London: Adam and Charles Black, 1971.

Barth, Markus, "Ephesians," *Anchor Bible,* Garden City: Doubleday, 1974.

Baugh, S.M., "A Foreign World: Ephesus in the First Century," in Andreas J. Köstenberger, Thomas R. Schreiner, and H. Scott Baldwin (eds), *Women in the Church: A Fresh Analysis of 1 Timothy 2:9-15,* Grand Rapids: Baker, 1995, pp. 13-63.

Brauch, Manfred, *Hard Sayings of Paul,* Toronto: Hodder and Stoughton, 1990.

Brooten, Bernadette J., "Early Christian Women and their Cultural Context: Issues of Method in Historical Reconstruction," in Adela Y. Collins (ed), *Feminist Perspectives on Biblical Scholarship: Society of Biblical Literature,* Chico: Scholars, 1985, pp. 65-92.

Bruce, F.F., *The Epistle to the Galatians: A Commentary on the Greek Text,* Grand Rapids: Eerdmans, 1982.

Bwalya, Kelly, *The Life of Dr Wyson Moses Kauzobofa Jele. Missionary to Zambia,* Mzuzu: Mzuni Press, 2014, ^{2}2017.

Campbell, Douglas A., "The Logic of Eschatology; The Implication of Paul's Gospel for Gender as Suggested by Galatians 3:28a in Context," in Douglas A. Campbell (ed), *Gospel and Gender: A Trinitarian Engagement with Being Male and Female in Christ,* New York: T&T Clark, 2003, pp. 58-81.

Clifford, Anne M., *Introducing Feminist Theology,* Maryknoll: Orbis, 2001.

Conzelman, Hans, *A Commentary on the First Epistle to the Corinthians,* Hermeneia, Philadelphia: Fortress, 1975.

Dube, Musa, *Postcolonial Feminist Interpretation of the Bible,* St. Louis: Chalice Press, 2008.

Duling, Denis C., *The New Testament: History, Literature, and Social Context,* Belmont: Thomson Woodsworth, 2003.

Dupont-Sommer, A., *The Essene Writings from Qumran,* tr. by G. Vermes, Oxford: Basil Blackwell, 1961.

Fiedler, Klaus, "Gender Equality in the New Testament: The Case of St Paul," in Klaus Fiedler, *Conflicted Power in Malawian Christianity,* Mzuzu: Mzuni Press, 2016, pp. 160-177

Fiedler, Klaus, *Christianity and African Culture: Conservative German Protestant Missionaries in Tanzania.* Blantyre: CLAIM-Kachere, 1999.

Fiedler, Klaus, *Conflicted Power in Malawian Christianity,* Mzuzu: Mzuni Press, 2016.

Fiedler, Rachel NyaGondwe, Hoffie Hofmeyr and Klaus Fiedler, *African Feminist Hermeneutics: An Evangelical Reflection,* Mzuzu: Mzuni Press, 2016.

Fitzmyer, Joseph A., "Another Look at *kephale* in 1 Corinthians 11:3," *New Testament Studies* 35, 1998, pp. 503-511.

Fitzmyer, Joseph A., *Scripture, the Soul of Theology,* Nairobi: Paulist Press, 2005 (1994).

Flavius Josephus, *Josephus,* (trs) H. St. J. Thackery et al, Loeb Classical Library, vol. 2, Harvard: University, 1965.

Gaebelein, Frank E. (ed), *The Expositor's Bible Commentary with NIV,* Vol. 10, Grand Rapids: Zondervan, 1976.

Grenz, Stanley and D. Kjesbo, *Women in the Church,* Downers Grove: InterVarsity Press, 1995.

Grosheide, F.W., *Commentary on the First Epistle to the Corinthians,* Grand Rapids: Zondervan, 1983.

Grudem, Wayne, *Systematic Theology. An Introduction to Biblical Doctrine,* Leicester: InterVarsity, 1994.

Gundry, Robert H., *A Survey of the New Testament,* Grand Rapids: Zondervan, 1981.

Gundry-Volf, Judith M., "Beyond Difference? Paul's Vision of a New Humanity in Galatians 3:28," in Douglas A. Campbell (ed), *Gospel and Gender: A Trinitarian Engagement with being Male and Female in Christ,* New York: T&T Clark, 2003, pp. 8-36.

Guthrie, Donald, *The Pastoral Epistles,* Leicester: InterVarsity, 1984.

Hay, Alexander R., *The Woman's Ministry in the Church and Home,* Llandysul: Gomerian Press, 1962.

Hilker, Mary C, "Experience and Traditions: Can the Centre Hold?" In Catherine Milacugna (ed), *Freeing Theology: The Essentials of Theology in Feminist Perspective,* New York: Harper San Francisco, 1993.

Hooker, M.D., "Authority on her Head: An Examination of 1 Corinthians 11:10," *New Testament Studies* 10, 1964.

"Invocation of Isis," papyrus 1380, *Oxyrhynchus Papyri,* London: Egypt Exploration Fund, 1915, 11: 214-216.

Jewett, Robert, "The Sexual Liberation of the Apostle Paul," *Journal of the American Academy of Religion*, no. 47, 1979, pp. 53-87.

Johnson, Lewis, "Role Distinctions in the Church: Galatians 3:28," in John Piper and Wayne Grudem, *Recovering Biblical Manhood and Womanhood*, Wheaton: Crossway Books, 1991, pp. 154-164.

Kaiser, Walter C., *Correcting Caricatures: The Biblical Teaching on Women*, Grand Rapids: Zondervan, 1981.

Kantzer, Kenneth, "Proceed with Care," *Christianity Today*, 3.10.1986, p. 6.

Keener, Craig S., *The IVP Bible Background Commentary, New Testament*, Downers Grove: InterVarsity, 1993.

Koessler, John, "Wounds of a Friend: Complementarians," *Christianity Today*, vol. 52, no. 6, June 2008.

Koranteng-Pipim, Samuel, *Receiving the Word. How New Approaches to the Bible Impact our Biblical Faith and Lifestyle*, Ann Arbor: Berean Books, 1996.

Kroeger, Catherine, "The Apostle Paul and the Greco-Roman World Cults of Women," *JETS*, (Paul and the Cults of Women), March 1987, pp. 25-38..

Kroeger, Richard Clark, and Catherine Clark Kroeger, *I Suffer Not a Woman*, Grand Rapids: Baker, 1992.

Laird, Harries et al, *Theological Wordbook of the Old Testament*, vol. 2, Chicago: Moody, 1980.

Laws, Robert, *Reminiscences of Livingstonia*, Edinburgh: Oliver and Boyd, 1934.

McCracken, John, *Politics and Christianity in Malawi, 1875-1940: The Impact of the Livingstonia Mission in the Northern Province*, Blantyre: CLAIM, ²2000, ²2000 (¹1974, Cambridge University Press)

Mijoga, Hilary, "Bible and Church Growth in Malawi," *Religion in Malawi*, no. 8, 1998, pp. 27-33.

Mijoga, Hilary, "Gender Differentiation in the Bible: Created and Recognized," in Jonathan S. Nkhoma, *Significance of the Dead Sea Scrolls and other Essays: Biblical and Early Christianity Studies from Malawi*, Mzuzu: Mzuni Press, 2013, pp. 176-198.

Modupe, Owanikin R., "The Priesthood of Church Women in the Nigerian Context," in Mercy Amba Oduyoye and Musimbi R. Kanyoro, *Will to Arise: Women, Tradition and the Church in Africa*, Pietermaritzburg: Cluster Publications, 2006, pp. 206-219.

Mollenkott, Virginia, *Women, Men, and the Bible*, Nashville: Abingdon, 1977.

Mounce, William D., *The Analytical Lexicon to the Greek New Testament*, Grand Rapids: Zondervan, 1993.

Neall, Beatrice S., "A Theology of Woman," in Karen and Ron Flowers, *A Woman Place*, Hagerstown: Review and Herald, 1992.

Neusner, Jacob, *From Politics to Piety: The Emergence of Pharisaic Judaism*, Upper Saddle River: Prentice-Hall, 1973.

Neusner, Jacob, *Understanding Rabbinic Judaism from Talmudic to Modern Times*, New York: KTAV Publishing House, 1974.

Nichol, Francis D. (ed), *Seventh-day Adventist Bible Commentary*, Vol. 6, Hagerstown, MD: Review and Herald Publishing Association, 1957.

Nkhoma, Jonathan, *The Use of Fulfilment Quotations in the Gospel according to Matthew*, Zomba: Kachere, 2005.

Oduyoye, Mercy Amba, *Introducing African Women's Theology*, Sheffield Academic Press, 2001.

Okure, Teresa, "Women in the Bible" in: Virginia Fabella and Mercy Amba Oduyoye (eds), *With Passion and Compassion: Third World Women Doing Theology*, Maryknoll: Orbis, 1988, pp. 47-59.

Osiek, Carolyn, "The Feminist and the Bible: Hermeneutical Alternatives" in Adela Y. Collins (ed), *Feminist Perspectives on Biblical Scholarship: Society of Biblical Literature*, Chico: Scholars, 1985, pp. 65-92.

Paas, Steven, *Ministers and Elders: The Birth of Presbyterianism*, Zomba: Kachere, 2007.

Peerbolte, Bert Jan, "Paul and the Law: Introduction Course on Paul, NT 2 Class notes," *JMTC*, 2008.

Perriman, A.C., "The Head of a Woman: The Meaning of *kephale* in 1 Corinthians 11:3," *Journal of Theological Studies*, 45, 1994, pp. 602-622.

Philo, "Philo," F. H. Colson and G. H. Whitaker (trs), *The Loeb Classical Library*, Harvard University Press, 1949.

Phiri, Isabel Apawo, "The Church as a Healing Community: Voices and Visions from Chilobwe Healing Centre," Isabel Apawo Phiri and Sarojini Nadar (eds), *On Being Church: African Women's Voices and Visions*, Genève: World Council of Churches, 2005, pp. 29-46; also in Jonathan S. Nkhoma, Rhodian

Munyenyembe and Hany Longwe (eds), *Mission in Malawi. Essays in Honour of Klaus Fiedler*, Mzuzu: Mzuni Press, 2021, pp. 430-448.

Phiri, Isabel Apawo, *Women, Presbyterianism and Patriarchy*, Blantyre: CLAIM-Kachere, 1997, ²2000.

Pierce, Ronald W., et al (eds), *Discovering Biblical Equality: Complementarily without Hierarchy*, Leicester: InterVarsity, 2004.

Powers, Ward, *The Ministry of Women in the Church: Which Way Forward?* Adelaide: SPCKA, 1996.

Practice and Procedure of CCAP Synod of Zambia, Lusaka, 2012.

Punt, Jeremy, "Post-Apartheid Racism in South Africa: The Bible, Social Identity and Stereotyping," *RT* 16, nos. 3-4(2009), pp. 246-272.

Rakoczy, Susan, *In Her Name: Women Doing Theology*, Pietermaritzburg: Cluster, 2004.

Richardson, Larry, "How does a Woman Prophesy and Keep Silence at the same Time? (1 Corinthians 11 and 14)," in Nancy Vyhmeister (ed), *Women in Ministry*, Berrien Springs: Andrews University Press, 1998.

Robertson, Archibald, and Alfred Plummer, *First Epistle of St. Paul to the Corinthians. The International Critical Commentary*, Edinburgh: T&T Clark, 1963.

Ruether, Rosemary Radford, *Women and Redemption: A Theological History*, Minneapolis: Fortress, 1998.

Scroggs, Robin, "Paul and the Eschatological Woman," *Journal of the American Academy of Religion* 40, 1972.

Seventh-day Adventist Bible Commentary, Hagerstown: Review & Herald, vol. 6, Acts to Ephesians, 1980.

Slee, Nicola, *Faith and Feminism: An Introduction to Christian Feminist Theology*, London: Darton, Longman & Todd, 2003.

Snodgrass, Klyne R, "Galatians 3:28: Conundrum or Solution?" in Mickelsen, *Women*, 1987, pp. 161-167.

Stagg, Evelyn and Frank, *Women in the World of Jesus*, Edinburgh: Westminster, 1978.

Taylor, Joan E., "The Woman ought to have Control over her Head because of the Angels (1 Corinthians 11:10)," in Douglas A. Campbell (ed), *Gospel and*

Gender: A Trinitarian Engagement with being Male and Female in Christ, New York: T&T Clark, 2003, pp. 37-57.

Tertullian, *De Corona 4. The Ante-Nicene Fathers,* Alexander Roberts and James Donaldson (eds), Grand Rapids, vol. 3, 1973.

Update of the Life and Work of the CCAP Synod of Zambia," A report presented to Presbyterian Church United States of America (PCUSA) Congregations and Outreach Foundation, September to November, 2014.

van Wyk, Jurgens Johannes, *The Historical Development of the Offices according to the Presbyterian Tradition of Scotland,* Zomba: Kachere, 2004.

Vyhmeister, Nancy Jean (ed), *Women in Ministry: Proper Church Behaviour in 1 Timothy 2:8-15*, Berrien Springs: Andrews, 1998.

Walker, William O., "The Theology of Women's Place and the Paulinist Tradition," *Semeia* 28, 1983.

White, Ellen G., *The History of Redemption,* Seoul: Everlasting Gospel Publishing Association, 2008.

Witheringstone, Ben, *The Paul Quest: The Renewed Search for the Jew of Tarsus*, Downers Grove: InterVarsity, 1998.

Internet

Aldrete, Gregory S., www.the greatcoursedaily.com, [18.8.2020].

Bamanie, N., "Women in Ancient Greece," 2016, www.researchgate.net/profile/Nuray_Bamanie.

Baskin, Judith R., "Women in Rabbinic Literature," www.myjewishlearning.com/beliefs/Issues/Gender, [16.8.2016].

Cartwright, Mark, "Ancient Greek Society," 2018, www.ancient.eu/article/483/ancient-greek-society.

Cartwright, Mark, "Women in Ancient Greece," www.ancient.eu/article/927/women-in-ancient Greece/2016.

Evans, Amanda, "Women in the Greek and Roman Perspective," 2003, http://housatonic.net/faculty/ABALL/PrimarySourceDocs/168.htm, [16.8.2016].

Larson, David R., www.religioustolerance.org/hom_bibg.htm, [17.8.2015].

Narrowe, Judith, "The Role of Women in Jewish Religious Education," July 2000, http://www.wcc.coe. org/wcc/English.

Papazov, Svetlana Renee, "The Place of Women in the Graeco Roman World," Texas, p. 2, http://enrichmentjournal.ag, [16.8.2016].

Rich, Tracey R., "The Role of Women, " p. 1, www.jewfaq.org/copyright.htm, [19.4.2015].

Robertson, https://medium.com/stoicism-philosophy-as-a-way-of-life/thespartan-philosophy-of-life-f0731afdb039.

Stempmorlok, Laura, "1 Timothy 2:9, 10: Greco-Roman Women," http://thirdwaystyle.wordpress.com/author/laurastempmorlok, [15.8.2016].

Tetlow, Elizabeth M., "The Status of Women in Greek, Roman and Jewish Society," 1980, www.womenpriests.org/classic/tetlow1.asp [20.6.2017].

The Role of Women in Spartan Society," https://phdessay.com/the-role-of-women-in-spartan-society-to-the-battle-of-leuctra-371-bc/ [12.4.2017].

The Status of Women in the Hebrew Scriptures," www.religioustolerance.org/hom_bibg.htm, [19.4.2015].

www.ancient.eu>article>th [29.8.2020].

www.GreekBoston.com [18.8.20].

www.Pbs.org>romans>women, [18.8.2020].

www.thegreatcoursesdaily.com, [29.8.2020].

Index

Adam, 45, 74, 102, 137, 149
Adamic, 93
Administration, 20, 21, 148
Aeschines, 130
Aeschylus, 115
African women, 42, 50
African women's eyes, 50
Alexandra, 77
Ammonites, 71
Ancient Greece, 52, 57, 154
Ancient Mediterranean, 128
ancient women, 83, 101, 144
androcentric, 111
androgyny, 94
Aristotle, 54f, 58, 93
Artemisia, 136
Artemision, 135
Asia Minor, 130, 135f
Athena, 52
Athens, 52f, 55, 78, 130
Augustus, 61f, 64
Autonomy, 51
Babylon, 68
Babylonian Talmud, 66, 69, 71, 73
Bacchiocchi, Samuele, 11, 101, 109, 116-118, 125, 131, 148
Bachelor of Theology, 28
Banda clan, 15
Banda, Gertrude Nyirenda, 27
Banda, Oswald Jimmy, 69
Bandawe, 15
Barbarians, 80
Baskin, Judith, 66, 73-75, 154
Bemba, 16
Bible, 9-11, 18, 41f, 45, 49f, 69, 75, 80, 83, 89, 95, 97, 105, 109, 112, 117f, 124, 127, 132, 134f, 144f, 148-153
Binary Couplets, 93
Bisa, 16

Blantyre Presbytery, 16
Bona Dea, 65, 98
Brauch, Manfred, 125-127, 131, 134, 149
Bruce, F.F., 88f, 149
Caesarea, 73
Cape Maclear, 15
CCAP leaders, 49
CCAP Synod of Livingstonia, 7, 19, 148
CCAP Zambia, 5, 6, 10, 12- 49, 87, 90f, 96, 113, 142-148
CCAP Zambia women, 41
Central Africa, 5, 7, 10, 14-16, 19f, 147f
Central Province, 15
Ceres, 65
Chasefu, 10, 16, 19, 27, 29, 38, 44, 144, 147f
Chasefu South, 38
Chasefu Theological College, 10, 27, 29
Chastity, 65
Chewa, 16
Chibambo, Lucy, 19, 148
Chibambo, Wedson, 19, 148
Chikhokho, 15
Chilenje, Victor, 15f, 18, 147
Chipata, 15, 22, 26, 33, 42, 45, 47, 148
Chipeta, Rev Thandiwe Theu, 24, 26f, 148
Chitambo, 14, 16
Chitheba, 16
Christ Jesus, 21, 30, 84, 86, 88, 92, 94f, 103, 141
Christendom, 140
Christian code, 92
Christian liberty, 97

Christianity, 9, 11, 14, 42, 66, 72, 78, 80, 84f, 89-91, 97, 107, 118, 120, 128, 149, 150f
Cicero, 116, 135
Clark Wire, Antoinette, 84
Clifford, Anne, 19, 149
Commentators, 80
Community Schools Department, 18
Complementarians, 11, 151
Congregations, 6, 17, 154
Conservative, 85, 149
Copperbelt, 22, 24, 28, 31, 33
Corinthian Christians, 105, 110
Corinthians, 79, 82, 90, 98-121, 124, 143, 149f, 152f
Cults, 82, 98, 115, 129, 144, 151
Culture, 40-42, 51, 59, 65, 85, 148f
Cybele, 115, 130
Cynics, 56
Daka, Rev Naomi, 29f, 145, 147
David Livingstone Presbytery, 30
Delphi, 130
Demeter, 115, 130
Diana, 134
Dionysian frenzy, 115
Dionysian religion, 116
Dionysos, 98-100, 115f, 130
Dodona, 130
Eden, 74
Edomites, 71
Egalitarianism, 11
Ekwendeni Lay Training Centre, 20
Elders, 16f, 152
Eleusis, 130
Emusa CCAP Congregation, 38
Ephesian churches, 10, 132
Ephesian Tale, 135
Ephesians, 10, 75, 135, 149, 153
Ephesus, 31, 100, 130-140, 149
Epiphanius, 137
Epistle to the Galatians, 79, 82, 89, 149

Equality, 10, 34, 89-91, 97, 128, 149, 153
Eschatology, 81f, 94, 145, 149
Essenes, 76
Etieocles, 115
Evans, Amanda, 51f, 60, 154
Eve, 45, 74, 102, 137
Eve's part in creation, 137
Executive members, 6, 33
Fadyen, John M., 14
Fiedler, Klaus, 5, 10, 85, 89f, 97, 149f, 153
Fiedler, Rachel NyaGondwe, 5, 41f, 45f, 96f, 113, 143, 145, 147f, 150
Galatia, 80, 98
Galatians, 10, 11, 28, 30, 32, 79-97, 103, 113, 145f, 149-151, 153
Gallo-Graecians, 80
Gauls, 80
General Assembly, 14
General Secretary, 6, 19, 21, 24f, 28f, 32, 39, 41, 44, 147
Genesis, 50, 102, 125
Gnostic Christians, 107
Gnostic ideas, 136
Gnostic male, 107
Gnostic position, 108
Gnostic teaching, 107
Gnostic views, 128
Gnostic women, 107
Gnosticism, 129-131, 134
god's frenzy, 99
Gospel of Thomas, 137
Government of Zambia, 44
Grecian custom, 115
Greco-Roman cults of women, 82
Greco-Roman world, 82f, 98, 111, 115, 144
Greece, 51, 56f, 78, 115, 130, 154
Greek myths, 135
Greek priestesses, 65
Greek religion, 130
Greek women, 51f, 56f, 68, 105

Greeks, 55, 136
Grudem, Wayne, 80, 88, 90f, 144, 150f
Gundry-Volf, Judith M., 85-87, 145, 150
Guthrie, Donald, 132, 150
Halicarnassus, 136
Headdress, 101, 104, 113
Hellenism, 78
Hellenistic ideology, 93
Hellenistic queens, 61
Hercules, 98, 136
Herod the Great, 68, 77
Hipparchus, 56
Historical-Critical Method, 11
Hittites, 71
Horace, 135
Inclusiveness, 25, 86f, 95f, 113, 138, 140, 142f
Inclusiveness, 145
interpolations, 106
Interpretation, 89, 144, 149
Isis, 136, 150
Israel, 73, 75, 123
Italy, 130
Jerusalem, 80
Jesus Christ, 32, 79, 88f, 103
Jewett, Robert, 96f, 144, 151
Jewish courts, 77
Jewish Torah, 89
Jewish women, 65, 69, 71f, 74, 99, 104, 139
Jews, 68, 70, 72, 80, 140
Johnson, Lewis, 80, 88, 151
Joseph, 77
Josephus, 76, 77, 150
Judaism, 65, 67-80, 102, 134, 152
Judaizing, 81
Julia, 62
Justo Mwale Theological University College, 7, 25, 28, 147
Kabandama, 6, 24, 28f, 39, 44, 147
Kamoto, 16

Kapunda Banda, 15
Karonga District, 15
Kasungu, 15
Kazembe, 16
Keener, Craig, 69, 105, 117, 132, 151
Khondowe, 15
Kirk session, 16f
Koyi, William, 15
Kroeger, Catherine Clark, 82, 98, 100, 115, 129, 136, 144, 151
Kroeger, Richard Clark, 151
Kwacha CCAP Congregation, 39
Lake Nyasa, 14
Lala, 16
Laws, Dr Robert, 14, 16, 151
Laws, Mrs, 15
Leadership, 5, 13
Liberation, 89, 96, 144f, 151
Literalistic interpretation, 28, 142, 146
Literature, 5, 7, 66, 74f, 79, 98, 102, 109f, 118, 134f 145, 148f, 152, 154
Livingstone, Dr David, 14, 30
Livingstonia Mission, 14f, 151
Livingstonia Synod, 16, 20f, 25, 148
Lovedale, 14f
Luanshya CCAP Congregation, 28, 35, 39, 145, 148
Lubwa, 16
Luke, 134
Lundazi, 15f, 18, 21, 25-27, 29, 31, 36-38, 41, 43f, 144, 147f
Lusios, 99
Lydian queen, 136
Magna Charta of Women, 96, 144
Malawi, 2, 7, 9f, 14f, 20f, 67, 69, 128, 133, 147, 151, 153
Malenga Mzoma, Chief, 15
Marambo (Eastern Province), 15
Marriage, 59
Mary, 48, 137, 139, 150
Masculinity, 83
Mazabuka, 29f, 145, 147
Mechitzah, 66

158

Midlands, 44
Mijoga, Hilary, 9, 95, 127f, 138, 145, 151
Minister of Word and Sacrament, 26
Mithras, 98
Mitzvoth, 69
Moabites, 71
Modupe, Owanikin, 49, 151
Moses, 109, 123
Mponda, Chief, 15
Mtonga, Betty Mvula, 18, 26
Mwenzo, 16
Mystery cults, 65
Namalambe, Albert, 15
Namwanga, 16
Narrowe, Judith, 69, 154
Ndola, 31
New Testament, 5, 7, 10, 31f, 69, 75, 78, 89f, 97, 103-105, 110, 113, 117f, 123, 125, 129, 131f, 141, 143f, 148-152
Ngoni, 16
Ngulube, Simon K., 16
Nicolaitans, 137
Nkhata, Catherine Mazunda, 18
Nkhoma, Jonathan, 5, 70, 95, 127, 145, 151
Nkhoma, Rev Kondwani, 22-26, 35, 37, 147
North Africa, 104
Northern Province, 14f, 151
Ntintili, Mapasa, 15
Nyirenda, Rev Susan (nee Tembo), 28, 35, 145, 148
Oduyoye, Mercy Amba, 49f, 151f
Okure, Teresa, 50, 152
Old Testament, 73, 102, 109, 118f, 123, 125, 151
Olylygia, 115
Olylygos, 115
Omphale, 136
Ordination, 18, 25
Orpheus, 98

Osiek, Carolyn, 134, 152
Osiris, 115
Panathenaea, 52
Papazov, Svetlana, 59, 66, 71f, 155
Pastoral care, 35
Pastoral counselling, 35
Patriarchy, 41, 153
Patricians, 60
Paulinists, 118f, 154
Pergamum, 137
Peter, 137, 140
Pharisees, 71, 75f, 101, 110, 152
Philo, 68, 152
Phiri, Isabel Apawo, 41, 49, 152f
Plato, 53f, 78
Plebeians, 60
Plutarch, 55, 57f, 115
Polias, 52
Powers, Ward, 82, 90, 92, 103, 124, 153
Presbyterian, 5, 7, 10, 14, 15-17, 19f, 25, 96, 147f, 154
Presbyterian polity, 17
Presbyterianism, 17, 41, 152f
Presbyteries, 6, 16, 18
Presbytery Clerk, 29
Presbytery meetings, 24
Presbytery Moderator, 23, 26-28, 37
Priesthood, 49, 151
Qumran Community, 75f, 149
Radical Jew, 84
Rakoczy, Susan, 19, 153
Respectable women, 51
Rich, Tracey, 66, 68, 70, 155
Richardson, Larry, 103, 153
Riddel, Alexander, 14
Robertson, 57, 155
Roman Corinth, 111
Roman Empire, 61, 77, 104
Roman era, 74, 116
Roman law, 59, 61
Roman matrons, 130
Roman province, 80

Roman women, 59-61, 63f, 78, 99
Romans 16, 115, 120
Sabazios Cult, 130
Salamis, 136
Salome, 137
Sappho, 58
Satyr pants, 100
Scroggs, Robin, 103, 107, 153
Second Temple, 68
Senga, 16
Sessions, 18
Sexuality, 83
Sham man, 100
Sidonians, 71
Silence, 103, 106, 108, 120f, 153
Simpson, Allan, 14
Siwale, Euwen, 16
Slee, Nicola, 19, 153
Socrates, 54, 78
Solomon, King, 71
Solon's Code, 52
South Africa, 7, 14f, 25, 83, 153
Southern Tanzania, 15
Sparta, 56-58
Staffing Committee, 39
Status of Women, 52-55, 58, 61-63, 65, 68, 76f, 155
Stempmorlok, Laura, 52, 60, 155
Stephanas, 122
Strabo, 115, 136
Submission, 89, 102, 113, 122, 127, 133f, 140, 143
Subordination, 60, 78, 104, 108, 120, 122, 125
Synagogue, 99
Synod executive, 18, 31
Synod leaders, 31f, 35, 48, 145
Synod leadership, 29, 49
Synod meetings, 17, 24
Synod of Zambia, 10, 17f, 153f
Synod offices, 33

Systematic Theology, 90f, 144, 150
Talmud, 66, 71, 73
Tamanda, 16
Tarsus, 81, 99, 104, 111, 154
Taylor, Joan E., 111, 113, 120, 143, 153
Temple ministry, 77
Tertullian, 104, 154
Tetlow, Elizabeth M., 52-56, 58, 61-63, 65, 76, 77, 155
Thales, 78
Theology, 5, 9, 19, 29, 36, 45f, 48-50, 67, 79, 118, 141-154
Thesmophoria, 98
Timothy, 24, 52, 60, 79, 82, 90, 124, 129, 130-132, 135f, 138f, 149, 154f
Torah, 69, 71, 73, 119
Tradition, 17, 48f, 96, 108, 118, 150f, 154
Tumbuka, 16, 18, 113
Umanyano, 18
Univiri, 65
Uyombe, 16
van Wyk, Jurgens Johannes, 17, 96, 154
Vestry, 18, 43
White, Ellen G., 74, 154
Wives, 55
Women in Holy Ministry, 22
Women leadership, 13
Women Prophets, 84
Women Theologians, 45f, 147
Women's submission, 133
Women's subordination, 60
Xenophon, 58, 135
Xerxes, 136
Young, 15
Young, E.D., 14f
Zambia School Certificate of Education, 44
Zomba Theological College, 22

www.ingramcontent.com/pod-product-compliance
Lightning Source LLC
Chambersburg PA
CBHW010832230426
43668CB00019BA/2417